ACCOLADES

Patti Lustig has written a high-impact book that's equal parts memoir and self-help. She takes us on the journey of her life, exposing her most vulnerable moments, then strengthens us to overcome our own challenges. A must-read for anyone who is looking for hope."

– Nancy Erickson, owner, The Book Professor®

The journey Patti takes us on runs the gamut from laughing out loud to screaming out loud, "No! That is not true!" to cheering on her successes. This book is a thoughtful, thought-provoking, piece of art. I especially appreciated her relevant insights on how to bring about change and growth in our personal lives. This is a worthwhile read."

– Karen Koven, Poet and Published Author

Patti Lustig uses the realistic, no BS stories from her life in a way that makes you wonder, "How did she turn out so incredibly empowered and happy!?" There's no sugar-coating Patti's experiences — she tells us stories that make us reflect on our own lives and inspires us to keep moving through our own challenging places. If you're a woman who has lived a life that's either exhausted you, made you feel like you don't have control, or caused you to wonder "what you did wrong" — please read Patti's book. You'll feel inspired and realize that you seriously have the power to create whatever life you're dreaming of!"

– Jen Liddy, Business Development Coach

There is always someone who has walked in your shoes who can show you the way. Patti is one of those wise women. I've known Patti for over 20 years and have called on her for guidance multiple times. Her recent work with PSYCH-K® is life changing. I love that her new book *Odyssey of a Woman* is loaded with great advice and practical hands-on guidance for anyone seeking to live a magical life on their terms. I love this book!

– Tonja Waring, Entrepreneur, Single Mom

In this moving memoir, the vicissitudes of Ms. Lustig's life are relatable to every woman's journey...complete with friends and foes, doubts and determination, setbacks and successes. Fiercely pursuing her best life, she transforms herself through wisdom she discovers along the way and becomes an example of empowerment for others.

Kelley Hails, MD

ODYSSEY OF A FEARLESS WOMAN

How you can meet life's challenges
with courage and spirit.

For every woman fighting to find her power, reignite her passion, and live her most authentic life. For every woman who thinks she's too damaged, beaten down, or too old to still make a difference.

Mostly, for my beautiful daughter, Matilda, so she never forgets that she has the inner strength to bring herself back from anything life throws at her.

CONTENTS

Baby's Silent Night

It is cold outside in Lawrence, New York, a small town near the Catskill Mountains. It's the evening of December 19, 1952, and we live on a chicken farm. Dad is sitting in front of the TV with his vodka and tonic. Mom's about to burst from her swollen belly. She wonders if I will arrive on Christmas Day, the same as her eldest child, Peggy, who is turning eleven. If that happens, she will have two sets of children born years apart on the same day, just like her second and third children, Maureen and Tom, who were both born on June 7th only two years apart.

Mom didn't plan on having another child.

I am an accident.

She pinpoints the exact moment it happened – one spring night when the monotony from the lingering snow and chill weather (and the kids staying at the neighbors) drove her husband and her to express some distant passion they held for one another long ago. She remembers it as a sweet experience but never imagined it would produce a child; she was forty, after all.

Her husband (my father), Francis, is angry about the pregnancy because the farm has been struggling for years and another mouth to feed adds more burden.

That night, Mom made a huge pot of soup to tide them over for several days in case I come early. She sleeps fitfully and awakes at six in the morning, realizing the bed sheets are sticky and wet. Her water has broken, and she hollers for Francis to come and take her to the hospital. The kids are just stirring, and Peggy is told to wake them, ready everyone, then wait until Dad returns to pick them up.

Tom, the eight-year-old, is most excited. He has been telling everyone for months that I am a boy. In fact, my name, Patrick, has already been chosen. The kids and Francis wait and wait with anticipation at the hospital, and at 11:30 a.m. on December 20th, I make my entrance. Mom is so happy, along with my sisters, Peggy and Maureen. Dad is relieved that Mom and I are in good health, but Tom? He is sooooo mad. He wanted a brother.

I am renamed, Patricia Joy.

As soon as Dad returns home with the kids while Mom and I stay at the hospital, Tom runs away. No one worries that much because they figure he'll be back when he gets hungry, and indeed he returned around dinner time huffing and puffing around the house, giving everyone the silent treatment.

Thus, my adventure began.

INTRODUCTION

*"The difference between successful people and
others is how long they spend time
feeling sorry for themselves."*

Barbara Corcoran

Whatever age you are, you are either going through, have gone through, or can see on the horizon a major life transition. This is the nature of life. When you stop dealing with life transitions, you will probably be dead.

You may feel afraid, frozen, confused, and lonely.

I understand. I've been there many times in my life.

A new direction is not as hard as you think to weather these storms and re-emerge victorious and stronger than when you started. The stories of my life are meant to teach, inspire, and motivate you to determine what you need, provide the support necessary, and take the actions to transform your circumstances.

You can live a miraculous life no matter where you have been or what you are going through. You will find access to all the elements necessary to reinvent yourself and your life in the stories, as well as practical exercises in the second half of the book. By engaging in them, you will be able to reinvent your life and find the strength and courage to keep striving to live your best life.

Many times, a book alone can help you move to the next level in your life, and other times, having a support structure will help you resolve what's keeping you stuck and empower you to get in action in a faster, easier way. If you are ready to make a change quickly and easily, visit my website at www.sagethink.com and sign up to treat yourself to a complimentary session.

I'd love to hear from you.

Warmly,
Patti Lustig.

CHAPTER 1

You've Got to be Kidding

"All the world is made of faith, and trust, and pixie dust."

J.M. Barrie, Peter Pan

I grew up in Dunedin, Florida, about thirty miles northwest of Tampa. In the fifties, it was a small town.

My mother moved our family which included my three siblings and me from upstate New York after my father decided to return to work in the Merchant Marines. This was all the reason she needed, so she packed everyone into our 1950 Chevy station wagon, and we headed to sunny Florida. I will be forever grateful to her for this.

I was two years old when we moved, and I have no recollection of living in the cold. For the most part, my childhood was idyllic. My older sisters left for college when I was six and my brother, who was eight years older, did his own thing. As a result, my mother and I were very close. I loved her so much. She always treated me special; taking me out to eat on Fridays and giving me little gifts on holidays. I remember one Valentine's Day; I came home to find a new belt, scarf, and blouse laid out on my bed. Actions such as these made me feel secure and loved.

In return, I tried to show my love for her by being the best daughter I could be. I excelled in school and often received praise from my teachers; I was a talented musician. My mother adored this because her mother was a talented singer on Broadway, and my mother played a mean piano. Because of my musical abilities, I was one of the few chosen to learn the bagpipes. I also participated in dance classes four times a week and won two dance scholarships. To top it all off, I attended church regularly.

The only dark spot in my life was my father, who traveled most of the time and was rarely home. When he did return, he wreaked havoc. He was an alcoholic and never went anywhere without his flask of vodka. He was controlling, psychologically abusive, and at times physically abusive.

My stomach still churns when I recall the memory of a time when he arrived home to learn that my brother had been thrown in jail again. My mother ran frantically from room to room, closing all the windows with the speed of a woman horrified that the neighbors would hear my father screaming at the top of his lungs.

The memory of his shouting still reverberates in my head, "You are a disgrace to this family, you will never amount to anything, and you should be ashamed to put your mother in a position like this!"

My father raised his arm to strike my brother.

In turn, my brother screamed at my father in a voice that was filled with anger, fear, and helpless regret, "You are nothing but a drunk asshole, and you don't control my life. Fuck off and die. I can beat your ass anytime I want to, and you'll be sorry when I get the chance. You don't care about this family; all you care about is your booze! I can't wait to turn eighteen and get the hell away from you!"

After observing this scene in fear and helplessness, I ran to our one and only bathroom. My legs propelled me away from the scene I did not want to witness. I locked the door, pressed my hands against my ears to muffle any sounds, and put my head down, waiting for it to end. My feelings were a jumble. I was scared of being physically hurt, angry that my father was so mean, scared for my brother's safety, and mad I couldn't do anything to help him. I waited and waited and decided that the only way to avoid being hurt myself was to keep my head down, never talk back or make waves, be a good girl and look forward to the day I could move away from him.

Thank God my father was away more than he was home. After this scene, my brother moved out. I was ten at the time, and my mother and I grew even closer. She became my best friend and confidant and I felt safe to tell her anything.

The first major transition in my life occurred in June 1967. My father had just retired at the age of sixty-two – an early retirement due to medical conditions. I was fifteen. My mother called me onto the porch and said, "Your father and I have made a decision. He has invited me on a trip around the world, and we will be sending you to live with Peggy."

I was in shock. Peggy lived in Buffalo, New York. I couldn't make sense of what was happening. I ran to the bathroom and threw up. I couldn't believe it. My mother, my confidant, my best friend, my safety net was abandoning me for *him*. It was unbelievable. What about my friends? What about my teachers, my church, and everything that was familiar to me? Everything and everyone were being ripped away from me.

The anticipation of the move sent me into a spiral of depression and anxiety, something I had never experienced before. I began to eat compulsively – entire bags of potato chips, quarts of ice cream, Little Debbie cakes, and whip cream sprayed directly into my mouth.

Over the year they were traveling, I gained sixty pounds and developed bad habits that haunted me for years to come. On top of that, my mother had a major phobia about being "fat." Her mother was obese and she spoke about weight gain as the absolute most horrendous thing that could happen to a person. I believe I gained this weight to shock her and to make myself feel safe.

I moved to Buffalo that August. Everything I dealt with was overwhelming and often scary. I was living in a tiny two-bedroom apartment with my sister, her husband, and their new baby. I attended the largest high school and had to ride thirty minutes each way on the city bus. I didn't know anyone my age and by October, it was dark by 4:00 in the afternoon and snowing, something I had no experience with.

A few months into living in Buffalo, I met some girls in my neighborhood who attended the youth group of the Unitarian Universalist Church on the comer. I joined up, and this became my new family. This allowed me to take my attention off the anger and resentment that I carried towards my parents and focus on new interests and activities. It was the height of the Vietnam War, and the church was active in the anti-war movement, staging demonstrations and bringing major musical talent in for anti-war concerts. It was electrifying to be part of this group, and I had a new purpose in my life.

How did I cope? The solution that made the greatest positive impact for me was connecting with like-minded people. Another step was to focus on interests and activities that filled me with newfound satisfaction. Even though I would have preferred to be at home in my Florida community, I got involved in my new situation and found ways to thrive. This allowed me to generate a closer relationship with my sister which remains to this day. In the second section of the book, I discuss various solutions that allow you to powerfully redefine whatever situation you find yourself in and begin to develop a new way forward.

CHAPTER 2

A Wrenching Decision

"You are the one that possesses the keys to your being. You carry the passport to your own happiness."

Diane von Furstenberg

After spending a year in Buffalo, now much to my chagrin, I had to move back to Florida. My sister's husband was only in Buffalo for a one-year residency; then, he was drafted and went to Vietnam. When my sister, her baby, and I moved, extreme anxiety began to seep into my daily thought process.

Again, I was devastated because I loved my new community, my school, my friends, and my connection to the Liberal Religious Youth at the Unitarian Church in Buffalo. I returned to Dunedin High School and immediately sought out and joined the Liberal Religious Youth at the Unitarian Church there.

I was still separated from my mother, as my parents were on another trip, searching for a place to retire. I found I couldn't relate to my old friends as I had become a radical hippy. My friend, John, and I had cars, and we skipped every day of high school we could and still meet the requirements to graduate.

I went on to attend the University of Florida in Gainesville, the alma mater of both my sisters. There had been no discussion about where I might want to go to college or if I wanted to attend. In those days, any Florida resident with at least a C average would be admitted. College was overwhelming! The massive lectures with over two hundred students left me confused; I tried my best but couldn't pass my classes.

I ended up on academic probation the first semester. I begged my parents to allow me to attend the local community college, but they were opposed. So, I didn't try at all during the second semester, and my grade-point average plummeted further. I told my parents I didn't want their money and I was planning to go to community college.

Community college was exactly what I needed. They had a philosophy that no one should fail. If your grade went below a C, the class was dropped but never put on your transcript. It took me four years, but I finished with a stellar grade-point average and was readmitted to the University. I was now in upper-division classes, which were smaller. I graduated with a 4.0 in Special Education.

During that time, I was in constant turmoil. I had low self-esteem. I was a compulsive overeater, always freaked out about my weight, moved every year, was disconnected from my family, and had no clue what I wanted to do with my life. I had a few boyfriends, clinging to anyone I sensed liked me. One of my boyfriends was Roy. He had long hair, a long bushy beard, was tall and buff, and rode a motorcycle. He seemed like a dream. I'll never forget the romantic nights we spent in the back of his enclosed van – which had a bed, of course.

With the doors open, we listened to the flowing river, gazed at the bright starlight, and made love under the influence of some sweet marijuana.

Roy and I were living in a large, six-bedroom house with five friends on a remote road. It was summer, and it was hot. I have to admit; I took speed often to keep up with my studies. One day I decided to mow the lawn high on speed. I got the lawnmower out, revved it up, and with tons of fervor began mowing the one-acre lot. Because of the heat, I was wearing flip-flops. All of a sudden, the mower was up, and my foot was under it. There was blood everywhere, but I didn't feel pain, just shock. I began yelling at the top of my lungs, but every car that passed had its window up and the air-conditioner on.

I hobbled to the neighbor's house, praying they were home. Luckily, they were home, and they rushed me to the emergency room. It wasn't until I was in their car that I felt the pain. And it was intense. They stitched me up at the hospital and sent me home with painkillers. By that evening, I was retching uncontrollably and had to return to the hospital, where they gave me a different medication. This did not help either, so I stopped the pills and endured the pain. However, the vomiting continued, sending me back to the emergency room two more times. The doctors were stumped, so they gave me a pregnancy test. You guessed it; I was pregnant at eighteen years of age.

Terrified and confused, and all I could think was, *I'm not ready to have a baby. I don't want to be a mother. I don't want to marry Roy. I have too much I want to accomplish. What am I going to do?* In 1971 abortion was illegal in Florida but legal in New York. I consulted with both of my sisters who lived in New York and after much consideration, I decided to have an abortion. They paid for everything and agreed to never tell my parents. I am so grateful to them for this. They flew me up, housed me, and nurtured me through the process. The agency I worked through had a thorough process of pre-counseling and post-counseling. I returned to Florida and never told my father.

I lived with Roy for another year, and I guarantee you that he was not ready to be a father. I don't know if this was right or wrong, but it's under the bridge, and I forgive myself. I have peace about this decision.

I am aware that some of you may judge me for this choice, but the point of the story is that I had a choice. This was not an easy decision but realizing that we have personal choices in all situations is an important part of living powerfully. There are positive and negative consequences for every choice we make, and we need to weigh our ability to live with our choices.

As in the first story, I used my people resources in the form of family and counselors to get through these transitions.

CHAPTER 3

Time to Grow Up

*"I'd rather regret the things I've done than
regret the things I haven't done."*

Lucille Ball

Two months prior to my college graduation, an enormous pressure to be an adult weighed me down. I remember feeling shaky, as much from my binge eating hangover as my impending fear of what adulthood would mean in my life. In retrospect, I had been working since I was seventeen and mostly supporting myself to make ends meet. But, I had somehow equated graduating with "getting my shit together."

I imagined having to find a high-paying and more professional job, losing weight, dressing up, and finding a long-term partner. All of this scared me because I wasn't at all sure I could, or would, be able to accomplish any of these things.

My relationship with my father was strained. Even though I had successfully avoided being directly accosted by him physically during my childhood, I always feared his judgment and I resented him for siphoning my mother's love away from me when I was fifteen and for always making me feel like a failure. Simultaneously, I was always hopeful that my father might be proud of me someday.

An example of this dysfunctional relationship with him centers around the time I was visiting my parents in their newly built home in South Carolina. It was chilly and I had taken a shower in the guest bathroom. I turned on the heater that was installed in the wall. After I dried off, I hung the towel on the towel rack which was oddly placed just above the heater.

My mother called me for dinner and as it was being served, we smelled smoke. My father hurried toward the smoke and found the towel on fire. After he quickly extinguished the fire he bellowed, "What's wrong with you? You could have burned the house to ashes! How could you be so stupid? You don't pay enough attention and you are always doing dumb things like this! When are you going to grow up?"

I felt the tears well up in my eyes and I struggled to hold them. I hated crying in front of my father (not that he would care). I felt the anger rise up in my throat and I thought to myself, "Why the hell would someone put in a heater that is under a towel rack and why can't he be happy that at least, I am alright?"

I didn't say this out loud, though, because no one could ever win an argument with him. You might wonder what my mother was doing during all this. Well, we finished dinner in silence. He drank too much vodka (again) and later passed out on the couch while I found the ice cream and ate the whole carton alone in my room.

My mother was a kind, openhearted, and loving woman who always wanted to do the right thing and look presentable to her friends and family. This was sometimes to the detriment of herself and her children. She didn't marry until she was twenty-seven years old and in the early 1940's she was called an old maid. She had been living independently in New York City and working as a registered nurse for many years. After marrying my father, having three children, and moving to a farm in upstate New York, she began to realize that her beloved husband was an alcoholic who found it difficult to shoulder the burden of supporting a growing family.

Mother was deeply religious and never would have fathomed divorce. So, she stuck out her marriage and was loyal until the end. She seemed helpless to intervene in my father's outrage and outbursts. After the fact, she would come to me and say, "He doesn't mean it. He's Irish and prone to drinking. I'm sorry he said that to you. Just ignore what he says. You know he loves you." I would reassure her that I was alright, and we would all go back to our pretense of being fine.

Graduating from college represented a new opportunity to prove that he was right and that, "I would never be successful in life." I was terrified I would be forced to run home and would require his help. Needless to say, I was afraid and very uncertain about how to proceed. I knew I didn't want to live in Gainesville for the rest of my life, and my family had all moved out of the state, so I had very few reasons to stay.

I worried every day and talked to everyone about it. I was acutely aware of what they thought I should do. My instinct was to move somewhere brand new, but I didn't know where. My sisters still lived in New York City and my brother in Boston, but they were eight-plus years my senior, and we weren't very close.

I wanted to prove that I could be truly independent and make something of my life without their help – that looked like a blurred image and I couldn't bring the picture into sharp focus.

One night, at a dinner party, I met a woman who had just returned to Florida after living and working in Los Angeles for a decade. She worked as a Special Education teacher in a small private school in Torrance, California, a town slightly south of Los Angeles. The more she talked about her life in California, the more I wanted to go there. Like her, I also had a degree in Special Education and wanted to teach in a private setting.

I remember her describing the beautiful ocean, amazing sunsets, funky people, and the nurturing and exciting work environment that the school offered. She described the children she worked with and the incredible difference she was able to make for them. I decided right then and there that I was moving to California. Yes, I knew where I needed to go. Every instinct I had spoke to me; I was going to work at that very school!

My boyfriend at the time, Phil, thought that it was an extraordinary idea and helped me make plans. He figured that he'd join me at some point. Phil was a renaissance man, ten years older than me. He lived in a trailer park and made a living by purchasing tools and other valuable items at garage sales and flea markets, cleaning them up like new, and reselling them. He loved openly and fearlessly. Our relationship was not monogamous necessarily; I knew he wasn't dating anyone else, at the time, at least. We were hippies who believed in free love, smoked pot, and pondered the mysteries of the universe. This resulted in a situation where he was open and excited about me moving away from him and he hoped to visit and perhaps move in with me at some point but in California.

I decided to visit my parents for a week immediately after my graduation, stay there for a week and then head on to the west. My excitement grew as the send-off approached. Phil helped me pack everything I owned into my '69 Volkswagen Bug – I mean everything by that! He was a natural-born organizer after living in a trailer with more junk than one can imagine, packed away in small nooks and crannies.

Before I left, I had a bike on the back, a guitar in the window, and the only space left was the driver's seat. Phil bid me adieu and off I went headed to South Carolina, where I spent an awkward, emotionally charged week. I yearned to feel close and comfortable with my parents and wanted to stay and wanted to leave, simultaneously.

My anxiety rose with every passing day, and I made up all probable reasons why I couldn't follow through with my plans. I only had eighty dollars cash, my car was too old to make it across the mountains, my friend, Laurie, might not have the same phone number or even live in California anymore, I might not get a job and I didn't understand why I was leaving a safe and loving relationship behind.

The night before I was scheduled to leave, I was in a panic and my mind was chaotic. The sun was about to go down and I wanted to talk to Phil. I didn't want to use my parent's phone, nor have them overhear my conversation, so I made up a reason to go into town. I drove straight to a phone booth and dialed the operator to make a collect call. It was getting dark and it was hot and suffocating in the phone booth. The sweat began to drip down my chest. I was praying that he was home and would answer the phone. He did answer and accepted my call.

"I've changed my mind. I'm coming back. I'm too scared. I don't have enough money and… and what if something goes wrong?" I rushed through my reasons, " Plus, I miss you and I don't know why I am going away. How will I live without you?"

There was silence on the line and finally, he spoke, "I know you are scared, and I miss you, too. In fact, a lot. However, you know there's no real future for you in Florida and I think you would regret not taking this chance while you are young to explore. We are just one decision away from a different life. Always. I know you will meet some great people because you are so open and so loving. I know you will find many lucrative job opportunities that you wouldn't find here, and I think this is what you need to do. You need to discover 'what's next' in your life. I will come out in about six months and who knows, I might want to move. I don't want you to come back. I want you to trust that whatever you need will be there when you need it."

I was moved. I was both, excited and scared when I hung up. Then, I realized a tear was rolling down my cheek – or was it the rain falling slowly? I drove back to my parent's house, finished packing, and gave my mother a kiss goodnight. I drifted off into a blissful sleep and awoke ready to go. Phil was one of many angels that guided me in my life, regardless of what I put in front of him.

It took a lot of courage to move over two thousand miles to a place I had never visited with only eighty dollars in cash and literally no place to live. It turned out to be the trip of a lifetime!

I drove from early morning until eleven each night. The first night, I stayed in a rest area where many others were sleeping and slept in my locked car. I had my pillow propped up in the driver's seat window and didn't get the best night's sleep.

The next night I connected with a single woman in the lobby of a motel, and we shared a room for ten bucks apiece and the third night I found a single room for ten dollars; living on the edge as we call it. Believe it or not, I had forty dollars left when I reached Los Angeles.

I had driven across the country once before with some college friends but this time, it was different. I noticed things I hadn't seen before. I'll never forget the experience of driving through the steep mountain ranges of the Sierra Nevadas. My Volkswagen Bug would slow to around ten miles per hour, large trucks would whiz by me, and I wondered if I might slip backward down the mountain at one point. I ate a PB&J sandwich during the day and stopped each evening at the Pizza Hut where I ordered the ninety-nine-cent, all-you-can-eat salad bar – best deal with the money I had. This made me feel close to Phil as it was a tradition for us to stuff ourselves at least once a week in this manner.

Luckily, my mother had slipped me a Texaco gasoline credit card right before I departed because I had to replace all four tires when I was halfway to my destination. Just as Phil said, what I needed had been given to me and would present itself to me.

Each day made me feel as though I was getting closer to a new life, new experiences, and more exciting possibilities. I felt as if the whole world was opening itself up to me! I yearned to see what the next moment would unfold. On the evening of the fourth day, I reached Van Nuys, California, and called my old college roommate, praying I had an accurate phone number. When she answered I nervously said, "I'm here in Los Angeles and I need a place to crash. Can I stay with you?"

Without hesitation, she exclaimed, "Sure, come."

She lived on a ranch in Malibu, where she was the caretaker and no one else was around. The morning after I arrived, I stepped onto the cliffs overlooking the Pacific Ocean and thought to myself, "Phil was right." The universe was supporting me in a grand fashion and I had made the right decision.

Many of the transitions we face in our lifetimes, evoke fear and take an enormous amount of courage in order to move forward in a new and uncertain direction. At this period of my life, I allowed the support of a close friend to catapult me forward and I relied on the faith I put in myself and the universe to provide what I needed when I needed it.

CHAPTER 4

Now What?

"If you don't risk anything, you risk even more."

Erica Jong

I lived in Malibu for three weeks. I found Los Angeles to be daunting, the sheer enormity of it overwhelmed me. I called it the concrete jungle. The first week I was there, I secured an interview at the school I had learned about from my friend in Florida.

However, when I arrived at the location in Torrance, I was overpowered by my impression of dirt and dearth. There were no trees surrounding the school, the playground was built on concrete, and the city seemed disgusting and gross. I didn't even get out of my car. Instead, I made a U-turn and headed back to the beauty of Malibu. I later realized that Manhattan Beach was five minutes to the west and would have been an amazing place to live, too.

In 1979 the country was in the middle of a recession and jobs were hard to find. Lucky for me, the government had created a program in 1973 called CETA, The Comprehensive Employment and Training Act, to train workers and provide jobs in public service. It turned out that I qualified for the program and there were positions open at the Boys Club in a small suburb of Los Angeles called Simi Valley. This was my first real job – it was post-college, and I was finally putting my degree to use acting as a reading tutor. There were six college students hired and that year we had a blast.

I was excited to have found a job in three weeks, as well as room boarding in a home. It didn't take long before I learned that Simi Valley, although it seemed a better fit for someone who grew up in a fairly small town, was a bedroom community – a small rural community filled with families. It did not have much appeal to a young, single woman in her twenties. However, the year went by quickly and was filled with fun and laughter, along with the types of challenges a lonely twenty-something experiences in a new and overwhelming environment, especially given I had become estranged from my family and was uncertain of my future.

I moved to the San Fernando Valley, a conglomerate of cities north of Los Angeles. I spent the year vacillating between staying and moving back to Florida. As the year's end approached, an impending sense of dread grew larger and more ominous within me. I didn't know where I would work, where I would live, or how would I be able to support myself. I was angry with my parents. There was no looking back. I was determined to make it on my own, but I lacked self-confidence. My weight gain in high school and subsequent issues with binging, food, and weight issues from my college years had left me feeling lonely, unworthy, and unattractive. In addition, my father's words, "Why are you so stupid, ugly, fat, etc..." were still lurking in my mind.

As my job approached the end of my contract, coincidentally my apartment lease was up. I decided to lease a private room in a home in the valley in an area that was less desirable than I wanted because my funds were low. This was common in the 70s and I looked at several options. Most of the ones in the areas I liked were too expensive given I had no long-term job possibilities and feared my income would run out. I moved to a neighborhood in the low-end area of the San Fernando Valley – Canoga Park, California.

I remember driving through the neighborhood and becoming more and more nervous. The streets needed repair and the yards of most people had old, rusted-out cars on them. The house with the room for rent was decent looking, and the room was temptingly large with an enormous bathroom. Jeff, the owner, was a short, unkempt, chubby man whose hair needed to be washed. A wave of his body odor slammed into me. But he was friendly, and I figured I would never have to see him once I got moved in.

When he showed me the room, it was dirty, smelled of cigarettes, and extraneous junk in boxes scattered around and the bathtub was filled with tools. He promised that the room would be painted soon, everything would be spotless, the boxes removed, and the bathtub emptied before I moved in. I reluctantly signed the lease and gave him a deposit.

I felt very uneasy and uncertain about the place, but I had to vacate the one I was currently renting in a few days. Looking back, I could see this was a time when I did not trust my gut and made a decision based on fear.

I traveled light and the room was furnished, so I arrived at moving day with all my belongings crammed into my Volkswagen Bug. I was devastated to walk into an area much worse than the day I rented it. The walls were marred and marked up, the carpet was stained, and the cloying aroma of smoke and whiskey permeated the air. Then, there was the bathtub caked with dust and still full of tools – the exact opposite of what was promised. My stomach dropped to the floor. I wanted to wail loudly, give up, beg my parents for help, and start driving back to my home in Florida. I had nowhere to live and needed to find a job ASAP.

The owners of the home were at work, so I walked to my car, got inside, and proceeded to scream and cry my eyes out. I didn't know what I was going to do, but I definitely wasn't going to stay there. In the midst of my despair, I remembered Alice.

A year prior, I met Alice at a drop-in therapy support group in Santa Monica. It was close to Thanksgiving. She knew I was lonely and had no family in California. She graciously invited me to Thanksgiving dinner. At the dinner, I met her amazing friends and experienced her phenomenal cooking.

Alice was attending the group because she was working through her issues around finding a mate and being estranged from her own family. We became friends that year. She was the one person that understood exactly what I was dealing with in regard to finding a new job and place to live.

In a desperate attempt to bring in some income, I had taken a job as a door-to-door salesperson selling encyclopedia Britannica. (This was long before the internet and Wikipedia.) It was August and the San Fernando Valley was HOT! I was rather shy of adults, being much more comfortable with children. It was a struggle every day to pry myself out of bed, dress professionally, knock on doors, and try to get strangers to let me in and buy a set of books. I think I made a very small number of sales.

One day Alice had said to me, "Anytime you need a break, here is where my spare key is. Please feel free to come in the house, have some tea and take a rest."

She lived in a beautiful home in an upscale area of the San Fernando Valley with her adorable Shih Tzus, Madel, and Shaina. That awful moving day, I took her up on her offer. When she arrived home, there I was, relaxing in the air conditioning, loving the dogs, and dreaming of staying forever.

When she heard my story, she insisted I march back over to the house I had rented, demand my money back, and move into her spare room. I did exactly what she said, and oh my God, what a miracle.

Alice was another angel in my life. She was a beautiful, talented, successful, creative woman who taught art in public school to middle school and high school students. She was five years older than me and truly an inspiration. She owned her own home, had a job that she loved, had two beautiful dogs, and loved to cook. All she needed was a partner.

Before I moved in, she was lonely; we began a long and amazing friendship that I will always be grateful for. We spent many weekends at the beach, the art fairs, sunning nude in her private backyard, hot-tubbing, and eating great meals together. She was so generous, that a month after I moved in, I came home to find an array of new tops laid out on the couch for me. This touched me deeply and reminded me of the times my mother would leave unexpected gifts much like those.

I had found a decent place to live, a job was next. I still wanted to work in special education in a private school but had no idea how to secure a job. I struggled each day with writing the perfect resume, writing the perfect cover letter, and fearing I wouldn't find a job because the country was experiencing a recession. I had a poor self-concept. One day while I was sitting on the couch watching television, a light bulb of inspiration went off in my head – I needed to come up with a creative strategy that made me stand out and had the people in the schools I want to work for curious and interested in me.

I immediately ran and grabbed the yellow pages. I listed all the names and addresses of all private schools in Los Angeles where I might want to work. Next, I redid my cover letter so that it expressed who I was and what I had to offer. And, obviously that I was different.

Then, I thought, what would make me stand out? Perhaps if I included an easy way to communicate with me? I came up with the idea of enclosing a self-addressed, stamped postcard with printed options on the back to be checked off and dropped in the mail with every inquiry. They could let me know they had no positions at the time, would have a position open at a certain time, or wanted to schedule an interview now.

I remember the rush of positive energy I had and the exhilaration from taking charge of my life. I ended up receiving postcards from ninety percent of the schools I applied to and was hired as a substitute for one month on the teen ward of a psychiatric hospital, then hired permanently at the end of that month to replace the teacher who had gone on vacation. Now, I had a wonderful home, a friend, and a job from which to launch the next phase of my life.

Alice and I lived together for several years and our support was mutual until Alice met a wonderful man with two young sons. They married and we parted ways. I was happy her dream of having a family had finally come true.

Being without a place to live or a job can be a very intense time of transition that many of us have or will face at one point in our lives. Sometimes these transitions are voluntary but often they feel beyond our control as in the course of a divorce or when a corporation does layoffs. It is easy to get caught up in the fear of what will happen or not happen in the future and it, again, takes great courage and faith to move forward and trust the process. I weathered this transition by accepting the support of another and thinking creatively. In the second section of the book, I will share some practical ways to move through this fear and get creative about your future.

CHAPTER 5

Burnt Out

"Change your life today. Don't gamble on the future, act now, without delay."

Simone de Beauvoir

After working at the psychiatric hospital for three years, exhaustion crept in along with a sense of being overwhelmed. The job was difficult. I worked on two units that held thirty teenagers in total. These were kids with extreme circumstances and difficult emotional issues. I had trained to work with developmentally challenged adults and this was a whole different ball game. These kids didn't trust adults and attempted to undermine our authority at every opportunity. I was not a very assertive person at the time and easily fell into being overwhelmed and at times threatened by their behavior.

For instance, there was a sixteen-year-old male, John, who had lived most of his life in and out of foster homes. His mother was a drug addict and had died of an overdose when he was ten years old. He had been molested more than once and exhibited signs of major depression. Sometimes he was charming, smart, and fun to be around but when he got depressed, he was nasty and scary. One day, he returned to class, from his therapy session with his psychiatrist. We were holding class in a small pink room with no windows. I was on the far side of the room, farthest from the door. He entered, was visibly distressed, and began disrupting the other students who were working quietly on an assignment.

I quietly asked him to please sit down and be quiet.

"Shut up bitch. I don't have to listen to you or any other woman around this place," he screamed at me.

A shiver of fear crept down my spine. He was big – very tall and heavy set. I needed to keep my cool and keep everyone safe.

I mustered my calmest voice, "John, please calm down. Everything will be alright. Just take your seat and we can sit and talk."

He was pacing back and forth in front of me and the others, his brow sweating, uttering, "Fuck, shit, assholes, I hate all of you."

I prayed that the staff outside the room would hear him and help, but this room was specially designed to mute sound. Then I made a mistake. I said, "John, if you can't calm down, I will have to give you some units (negative points) and you could lose your privilege of seeing your girlfriend this week."

Well, this took him over the edge. He grabbed one of the chairs, lifted it, and began smashing it into the wall over and over, yelling, "Fuck you, bitch." Now the staff heard something, yet by the time they had opened the door and restrained him, there was a hole of at least twelve inches in diameter in the wall.

These types of outbursts were common, although not always as extreme. Given the post-traumatic stress disorder I was carrying as a result of my experiences with my abusive father, I often found myself in the evenings and on weekends, reliving the stress of those moments. I did not see any practical way to manage myself or my students so that mutual respect and care were instilled in us all. I desperately wanted to provide a safe, therapeutic environment but went home every day feeling like I had failed. They had walked all over me again like I was their doormat.

I was twenty-eight years old. Along with my work stress, I was still struggling with my weight, self-confidence, and feelings of unworthiness. My mother had drummed into me the notion that fat people don't have the same opportunities in life. As a result, I imagined that if I lost weight and stayed thin, I would then find the love I desperately sought. Being skinny would make me worthy of the career I loved (not that I knew what that was). I just knew I didn't want to teach, and I wanted to make more money.

Over three years I had lost and gained sixty pounds at least five times. I found some new miracle diet – an easy thing to do in Los Angeles – stuck to it religiously, lost forty or fifty pounds in five weeks, and then gained it back as soon as I hit my goal. I had two or three intimate relationships during this time that all ended in heartbreak.

At that three-year mark, a number of things began to implode within me at the same time. I was struggling in my job, my boyfriend had broken up with me, and Alice was getting married and moving away. This reminded me of all the people who had left me in my life – my mom, my sisters, my boyfriends, and now my best friend, Alice. Thoughts that there must be something fundamentally wrong with me began to take over.

I had just come to the end of another diet that I thought was the answer to something. Of course, it wasn't. I seemed to think that if I got thin, I would magically meet my dream guy, get an offer for a perfect job, and feel so good about myself that I would never suffer again. None of this ever happened. In fact, without extra weight, I found myself more fearful and insecure and wondered if I would ever be able to manifest the life I wanted. Each time I hit my goal weight, I would begin to binge uncontrollably, consuming massive amounts of sugar and fat every day until I had grown back to an uncomfortable size.

During this time, I experienced incredible shame as people noticed my weight returning. Each time, I plunged into a deeper depression than I had experienced before. One night, I went out to dinner with my dear friend and colleague, Mary Ann, who had also just gotten engaged – which was another slap in my face.

Everyone around me was finding the love they wanted except me. It was our monthly Mexican food/margarita binge night, and we drank and ate more than I ever remember eating and drinking before. It appeared to be fun on the surface, but when I got home, I cried for hours. I couldn't envision a way forward in my life and I felt completely hopeless. I was seriously having thoughts of checking myself into a psychiatric facility.

The next day I remembered that two years earlier, during a similar bout of depression, I had picked up a book, *The Book of EST*. I'd heard about this crazy weekend training called, *Erhard Seminar Training* (EST) and decided to read it out of curiosity.

EST was a phenomenon in California at the time, started by a gentleman named Werner Erhard. The book was a reporter's blow-by-blow description of what happened in the EST Training from a participant's point of view. I remember spending all day Saturday and Sunday morning reading the book.

Alice was on a weekend trip with her fiancé, and I was jealous and lonely. The process described in the book was fascinating. As I read, I felt as though I was with the people, sharing in their problems, and applauding their breakthroughs. I realized at that moment that I didn't need to remain a victim of my past and my circumstances. That day, encouragement and inspiration blossomed within me.

Instead of sitting around, beating myself up for gaining weight and having nothing to wear (I always got rid of all my larger clothes when I was losing), I realized I had choices. I chose to go out and buy new outfits, I chose to stop berating myself, and I chose to embrace my body as it was.

It was a nice fall day, so instead of driving to the store, I decided to walk. It was invigorating. I walked the mile there, bought some clothes I felt good in, and walked back. I was present to what I was grateful for – the beautiful weather, the amazing home I lived in, the great friend I had in Alice, and what could be possible in my future. I don't remember how long I sustained this new attitude, but it disappeared at some point. I figured if a book could make a difference, during one of the lowest points in my life, doing the actual course might provide the answer.

The next day, I found the EST Center which was only five miles from my home. This seemed rather serendipitous. I walked in and was directed to see the Enrollment Manager, Jerry Baden. He ended up being another angel in my life for many years to come. I signed up for the training which took place a few weeks later. I had to think about what results I wanted out of my participation. I ended up writing that I either wanted to never have an issue again with my weight and/or I wanted to be able to lose weight easily. I ended up getting both results and many more.

Training took place over two long weekends that went from 9:00 am to 3:00 am each day. Yes, up to eighteen hours a day – you read that correctly. It also included three Wednesday evening sessions from 7:00 p.m.to 9:00 p.m in the evening. These occurred before the program began, in the middle of the training, and a session after the training ended. This was meant to be intense and confronting and it was! The first day began with the trainer coming up on stage and saying, "You are an asshole, and your life doesn't work."

Many people took issue with this statement, but I had hit bottom and was open to anything that shifted the way I thought about myself and my life.

We were asked to make some hardcore agreements, including not leaving the room between breaks, not eating anytime other than the meal breaks, not taking medication that wasn't prescribed by a doctor (like Tylenol for a headache), raising your hand to speak, etc. The purpose of the EST Training was: To rehabilitate your ability to experience living, such that those things you have been putting up with or trying to change, clear up in the process of life itself.

The design of the course was meant to drive up the experiences that each of us had suppressed to survive. We were meant to move from living a life of survival to living a life of responsibility where we were able to generate what we desired. It was one of the hardest, yet most satisfying experiences in my life. I often wanted to bolt from the room. The only thing that kept me there was the promise I had made to complete it no matter what.

There were a number of times during the four days when I literally threw up (we were given barf bags.) I was confronting everything I was swallowing down with food and overeating – my feelings about being abandoned at fifteen, my anger towards my father, my sadness about being estranged from my family, my feelings about losing Alice to a man, my anger at the teens I worked with and the system, and more. I realized I was not allowing myself to *feel* and *live*, and that I also found it difficult to express my feelings to others.

One epiphany from this transition was that I learned that holding grudges – not forgiving my mother for her choices – held me back from being responsible for my life. It cemented me in victim mode and that being a victim served a purpose. I felt safer, yet unsatisfied.

I walked out of the EST Training with a new attitude and outlook on my life. I discovered I had the ability to make things happen in my life, rather than hoping and waiting. I was excited to see what I was able to create, and I looked forward to the challenges. I had made a one-hundred-and-eighty-degree shift. I could hardly believe it.

My first commitment was to apply the principles I learned to how I approached my job and the teens I worked with. Oddly enough, a substitute teacher was working with me the week after the training when my boss was on vacation, and I now found comfort in confiding to her how the struggles and issues we had with the kids in the classroom and on the unit were impacting me.

She was amazing – another angel in my life – and had worked extensively with this type of student over the years. She introduced me to a system that had worked for her, and we began to implement it. When my boss returned, she was impressed and aligned with this implementation. It wasn't easy at first but with much perseverance, our classroom became the model for effective management and my experience of my job had transformed.

Regarding my weight, I decided to eat healthy – no crash diets – and I asked to take over the Physical Education program. This would ensure that I was exercising two times a day. I couldn't believe that I was willing to endure the insults and jeering from the teens for the opportunity to exercise regularly. It paid off. In the first year, I lost fifteen pounds without going on a diet and I was certain those fifteen were gone forever. I have been able to keep my weight stable for the past forty years.

I was also committed to transforming my relationship with my family, some of which you will read about in an upcoming chapter. An important first step was my decision to stop being angry with my mother for leaving me when I was fifteen. I began to take responsibility for my life being the way that it was. She and I reconciled, our closeness returned, and we spent many wonderful years of connection. One of my most treasured memories is cruising the Hawaiian Islands together when she was seventy-five years old, right before she died. What a treat.

A few years later, I was offered a job with EST, and I ended up working there for ten happy years.

Often people stay stuck in a job or relationship that's not working or behavior that is cyclical and destructive. This can be a function of not knowing what to do or feeling they have to remain where they are because they don't know how to survive any other way. In this situation, I trusted my instincts and took a risk. I figured the worst thing that could happen if the EST Training did not work, was that I had wasted two weekends and some money. However, I thought, "What if the best thing happened?"

Well, the risk paid off and my life was now on a new, exciting trajectory. Risking and trusting are two of the most critical skills to living a life where you move through transitions, learn from them, and find your way to the next chapter.

CHAPTER 6

He Died Too Soon

*"The act of forgiveness takes place in our mind.
It has nothing to do with the other person."*

Louise Hay

"Hello, Pat?" my mother said in a weak, shaky voice.

I answered, "Mom, are you OK?"

"Your father died in his sleep last night."

Stunned and silent a tear dropped from my eye, and I searched for the right emotions. It was surreal. Here I was, thirty years old, in the middle of a strained relationship with my father. I was clinging to the hope I could heal that relationship but in a moment all that was over.

I had recently written him a letter forgiving him for a number of grievances, with the intent of generating a new, closer, more intimate bond.

I was quite angry with both my mother and my father for abandoning me when I was fifteen years old by taking a trip around the world, uprooting my life, and sending me to live with my older sister in Buffalo, New York. I stayed mad at them for close to thirteen years and had recently reconciled with my mother and was ready to risk a relationship with my father.

After participating in the EST Training, I went to work on healing my relationship with my mother, forgiving her for leaving me when I was fifteen years old, and being straight about what I wanted from her. We began to share authentically again. I told her that I had gotten pregnant when I was eighteen and I was afraid to tell her and had subsequently gotten an abortion.

She cried and said, "I'm so sorry you didn't feel safe to tell me." Then she shared about her early life and the trauma of loving a man who turned out to be homosexual.

Two years later, after continuing to transform my relationship with myself (I learned to love myself, I lost weight and kept it off, I fell in love with my job, I found a boyfriend, etc.), I decided I was ready to tackle my relationship with my father. I started this process by writing him a heartfelt letter. In the letter I said:

Dad,

I think I understand how you came to be the way that you are. I know your father died when you were eighteen and I know this was a great loss to you. Even though you wanted to go to college, you felt it was your duty to support the family (your older brother was in college already), so you took a job with the Merchant Marines. This forced you to grow up quickly, abandon your dreams, and isolate yourself from your family.

I believe this severely impacted your self-esteem and being from a typical Irish background you had the propensity to use alcohol to assuage your pain. In addition, after you married Mom, had three children, and bought and ran the chicken farm in upstate NY, your sense of responsibility overwhelmed you and because you had not learned how to nurture yourself, you ended up in a spiral of shame and blame.

On top of that, when the chicken farm went belly up, your shame multiplied, and I think you chose to go back to sea because you just didn't know how to be intimately connected with your family.

What I need you to know is who you have been in my life is someone scary, distant, and judgmental and I forgive you for that. I love you and need you in my life and I appreciate everything you have done for me. Moving forward, I intend that we have a different kind of relationship. I don't need you to be strong. I need you to be vulnerable. I want to be able to share my successes and my failures and have your support and encouragement for both. I promise to give you the same. I look forward to who we can be for one another and our relationship moving forward.

Love, Patti

I inquired of my mother, "Did Dad get my letter?"

Mom replied again with a shaky voice, "Yes, he received it yesterday and wept with gratitude. Thank you for giving him that gift on the day of his death."

My Dad played eighteen holes of golf and went fishing, his two favorite activities. That night, he died in his sleep.

I hung up the phone and said to my partner, "Fuck him, he didn't dare to call me up and connect."

I was angry and not sure how to get over it. Given that my father had been in the Merchant Marines, traveling three or four months at a time my whole life, it was hard to imagine that this time he was gone and would never return. Many times, I had wished he was dead, but this was a huge blow, given I had chosen to forgive and rebuild.

A week later there was a memorial service. My mother flew my siblings into Tennessee for the service. I remember very little about it, but I do remember the week we all spent together afterward. It was the first time in twenty years we had been together without spouses and kids. At first, it was depressing. From my point of view, we had not been close for years, and we had a particular way of interacting that dictated we be stoic, not needy.

Being the youngest by ten years, my role usually involved going along with whatever. This time, I screwed up my courage and jumped in to lead. This was a major turning point in my life.

I got everyone together and I declared, "I am unwilling for us to hang out together for one week doing the 'Brady' thing pretending that we don't need each other and then going to different parts of the country to grieve all alone! I request we share with each other how we feel and what we need from each other to move through this transition."

It turned out to be a deep, extraordinary time for all of us. In a sense, our father's death resulted in us coming together in a vulnerable way we had never been able to achieve before. This is, in my mind, the biggest contribution the death of our father gave us. What a beautiful gift.

Grieving was still a difficult process. At the age of thirty, there were many aspects of my life that I still struggled with, and I hoped that healing the relationship with my father would be part of helping me get through those things. Now that he really was gone, I felt abandoned all over again and wasn't sure how to process this. I was still single and unsure of my ability to sustain a long-term, loving relationship. I had struggled with my weight for fifteen years and had just begun to make some real progress in that area and I wasn't sure what direction I wanted to take my career.

At the time of his death, I was in a somewhat serious partnership and struggling because it was playing out like past relationships, I was working at a job I no longer had a passion for, and I had self-esteem issues. This all seemed to stem from my relationship with my dad.

Now what? How did I resolve these issues? Sometimes I didn't feel like I could go on. One day I asked my friend, Alice, if she had any ideas for how to move through the emotional pain caused by my father's death, and she recommended a book called, *How to Survive the Loss of a Love* by Peter McWilliams." This is a small, simple book that discusses the variety of reactions that people experience because of the loss of love and provides numerous recommendations for coping with pain and achieving comfort. I began to focus on taking some actions in the book and my grief began to subside. In the meantime, I was continuing to participate with EST and growing, learning, and expanding every day.

The things that made the greatest difference in coping with my father's death were communicating with my siblings which brought us closer, reaching out to my friend Alice for support, and taking actions necessary to move forward in my life.

CHAPTER 7

Married with a Baby

"You can't be that kid standing at the top of the
waterslide, overthinking it.
You have to go down the chute."

Tina Fey

After my father died, I worked at my teaching job for a few more years and I became more involved with the work of the EST Training and my own personal growth and development. Eventually, I decided to go to work at Werner Erhard and Associates (renamed Landmark Education in 1996) and worked with them for seven years in Los Angeles.

I loved that job, and it was a bitch. We worked very long hours (twelve hours a day, six days a week) and were not paid enough. I'd been doing it for six years when I began to notice that on my days off, I was sad and lonely – wondering if I would ever find someone to share my life with. I remember I got off work on Saturday at 5:00 p.m., drove to Blockbuster and rented four movies, popped into El Pollo Loco for a box of chicken, stopped at the convenience store for ice cream, and arrived at my small studio apartment (a room with a bed, closet kitchen, and bathroom) where I plopped down with my food, turned a video on and eventually drifted off into a food coma.

All-day Saturday, I engaged in the same routine and as I watched movie after movie (crying through many scenes), I would say to myself, *When am I going to find someone to love and share my life with? Probably never. Maybe I should quit my job. I don't know what to do. I don't think I am attractive and what if I pick the wrong guy? I'm not any good at relationships. I'm doomed. I'm probably going to live my whole life alone.* Maybe you've been there.

One day my boss announced that he was creating a seminar for single women who wanted to get married. Well, I jumped at the chance to participate, and at the end of the series, I had designed a project to meet and marry the man of my dreams by the end of that year. My plan was simple and creative. I asked a friend who was married to phone up twenty-five men I thought were interesting and set me up on dates. A few of the men declined but I ended up with about fifteen dates and met one man that I fell hard for.

My friend had my schedule and asked the men who were interested to schedule a date with me through her. One man said he would prefer to call me and set up the date, so she gave him my phone number. He called and asked me to spend a Saturday with him riding bikes in Santa Monica, eating a meal at A Votra Sante (a vegetarian/macrobiotic restaurant), and sharing a nightcap in an Irish Pub as it was St. Patrick's Day.

I appreciated his take-charge attitude and accepted. He was tall, handsome, and attentive. The day was idyllic; 75 degrees in Los Angeles, great conversation, and fun all around. We dated exclusively from that point on, moved in together after three months, and were engaged to be married that December.

Truth be told, I knew before we got married that I should call it off but how do you cancel a wedding that you have bragged about and two hundred people have RSVP'd for? His willingness to take charge – one of the things that had attracted me to him in the first place – ended up being the thing I could not tolerate in him. He went from being very charming, loving, and supportive, to being extremely self-absorbed, controlling, and psychologically abusive.

He was determined to have a child and I made it clear that I did not want a child at our age (I was 39, and he was 44). We fought about this and did not resolve the conversation before we married. This was his third marriage; he had no children and within a few months I turned up pregnant even though I was on birth control. Now I'm married, knocked up, and too embarrassed to admit to my friends and family that I made a mistake.

The pregnancy was a difficult one and my husband was very clear on how it HAD to go. We were having a natural birth outside the hospital and there were certain procedures that must be followed. At the same time, there were times when what he wanted or needed took precedence. I'll never forget when I was nine months pregnant, and it was my husband's birthday. We lived in Los Angeles, and he wanted to go to a spa in Ojai, an area that has a steep elevation. I had gained sixty pounds due to a condition that caused me to retain water and I became more and more uncomfortable as we gained elevation.

About fifteen minutes from the spa, bile raced up my esophagus and I knew I would start barfing at any moment. I cried out to him, "Please turn around! I'm going to barf and the elevation is making it worse." He declined, kept driving, and assured me "Just breathe and focus on something else and everything will be alright." At that moment a swirling feeling of dizziness began in my head as I grabbed my purse, emptied the contents, and barfed straight into it. Immediately he started yelling, "Why couldn't you wait until we got there? Why do you have to ruin my birthday?" I began to cry and wished to go home – to get as far away from him as possible. We drove into the parking lot and when I got out of the car, I realized I had also wet my pants. He led me inside, looking dejected and I slowly got cleaned up. We had dinner and a massage but feelings of rejection, of being trapped and ashamed that I had allowed myself to marry this man, overwhelmed me. That was when I said to myself, *Growing old on my own might not have been so bad.*

Throughout my pregnancy I was gaining weight at an alarming rate and at each appointment with my midwife, my blood pressure was too high. I would have to lie on my right side for fifteen minutes to bring it down. We were all hoping and praying the baby waited for my due date and that our plans for a natural birth would not change. I was placed on bed rest for two months prior to the anticipated birth and when I arrived for my check-up five days before the baby was due, my blood pressure would not go down. After laying on my left side for over an hour I was instructed to call my husband and have him take me to the hospital immediately. I remember the fear and disappointment in his eyes at the prospect of having his child born at a hospital where he would lose control of the process.

We arrived at the hospital, and I was introduced to the doctor who would deliver my baby. He was like an angel from heaven! He made me feel so safe and cared for as he explained that my condition did not put the baby in danger but did put my life in danger. He said we could wait and monitor the situation overnight while we attempted to induce labor but if nothing resolved by morning, we would need to look at surgically removing the baby. I spent a sleepless night waiting and never felt labor pains. At 10 a.m.

the doctor arrived and informed us that my condition was getting worse, and he recommended we do a C-section ASAP. My husband was crushed! He hated Western medicine and was against me having an operation and his child being born that way, but he finally agreed. I'll never forget the relief when the doctor administered the Epidural. All the pain and pressure of the last nine months seemed to disappear, and I had a sense of enormous relief. The baby was coming and all I had to do was lay there and watch it happen.

When my sweet baby girl, Matilda (we named her before she was born after her great-grandmothers on both sides) was born, it was the best moment of my life! She was amazingly beautiful (and still is) with a long, amazing torso and incredibly graceful fingers. Her father was present and immediately began following the nurses everywhere to restrict them from doing certain things and make sure they did others. I'm sure they were not very happy.

I spent five days in the hospital and besides loving my daughter, I can say they were not pleasant. I was in an enormous amount of pain and my child would not latch on to my breast in order to get her much needed nutrients. She would take four painful sucks and be done. All the lactation specialists did not make a difference and my husband was freaking out because he was dead set against her being fed anything other than breast milk. She lost a pound before we left the hospital, but I guess she got enough sustenance from her four sucks every few hours. I was frantic because my nipples hurt so badly, but I had to feed my baby and I didn't feel I could go against my husband's wishes.

When I got home, I didn't know what to do. I couldn't go on this way. I tried "freezing" my nipples to no avail and was ready to feed her formula when the pediatrician came to my rescue. He told me to pump my milk and feed it to her in a bottle until my nipples healed. It worked! She was happy, I was happy, and he was happy.

Thank the Lord. So now what? I've got a newborn, a controlling husband, and no job.

At this point, I'm frustrated, lonely, and scared! What do I do? Any direction I ventured left me with feelings of embarrassment. My husband doesn't want to raise his child in Los Angeles (where he grew up) and wants to move to Minnesota (where he had been living for many years). The last thing I wanted was to move somewhere with cold winters, so I suggest we go to Florida and live in my mother's abandoned apartment until we got settled (which I figured would be about a month). So, we did.

The problem was after we arrived in Florida and he began looking for work, he came home and declared, "I can't take a job here because they pay a third of what I received in Los Angeles. You don't expect me to work for that little, do you?"

"Well, what are we going to live on?"

He replied, "I will keep looking until I find something that pays me what I am worth. Besides, I have that programming project I'm working on that will pay off soon."

As it turned out, the first year of our marriage (we lived in my mother's retirement community) we survived on credit cards and a small amount of money I brought in doing phone sales while he went to the gym every day and built a crawling track for the baby. My life had this incredibly oppressive weight and I struggled every day with the decision to stay or go. I wanted to go but worried about what that meant for my future and how it might impact my child. After a year with no health or car insurance and little money for anything other than subsistence, I called the company I had worked for in Los Angeles and they offered me a job in Minnesota. How ironic! This is where he wanted to live all along. Of course, he was ecstatic, and off we went.

Choosing to divorce, especially when there is a child or children involved, is one of the most difficult decisions for any woman or man to make. At that point in my life, my heart spoke to me, *You cannot live with this man.*

Yet, I feared how leaving him might affect the life of my child. At play also was my pride – I didn't want to admit this failure to others – and the fear that my husband might physically hurt me and/or our child. In the spirit of making it work, I needed the comfort of knowing I had given our relationship my all. Therefore, I engaged in therapy with him for over three years.

If you are experiencing a similarly difficult decision, I recommend you identify what structures will help you work through your thoughts and feelings and engage in those structures until you know you have exhausted every avenue and then make a choice and go with it.

CHAPTER 8

Divorcing the Bastard

"This journey has always been about reaching your own other shore no matter what it is, and that dream continues."

Diana Nyad

I arrived in Minneapolis, Minnesota with my daughter in tow on the last weekend in April 1994. My husband had gone ahead of us to look for a job. I drove into a blizzard and always wished I had made a U-turn and driven out.

Managing to make my way to my husband's best friend's home in North Minneapolis, only to learn the house was in one of the less desirable areas of the city dismayed me. Then, I found out we would be sleeping on a mattress on the floor in a run-down home that was being renovated. There were nails sticking out of the walls and dust everywhere. In an attempt to be brave, I wrote my husband a Dear John letter prior to moving in which I declared I had certain requirements he needed to meet if we were to live together in Minnesota.

Nearly two weeks after I delivered the letter, I got scared and asked him to forgive me – which ended up putting me in a vulnerable position when I arrived.

I started my job and he, his. A few weeks later, we moved into a lovely duplex in Linden Hills. It didn't take long for my husband's controlling and obnoxious ways to creep back, and it became harder and harder to tolerate being around him.

Then he lost his job for the third time since our relationship began. The reason was always a lack of communication on the other person's part. It was the last straw. I couldn't take the stress any longer. I decided to leave him, but I had to plan carefully. I asked a friend to help me load up on a day he was working, and I asked his best friend to meet him at the house that evening to make sure he was supported.

I was terrified. I had pictures in my head of him showing up at my friend's house and shooting me and my child. Even so, the option to stay another day was no longer one I was willing to choose. I phoned him that evening and I placed my cards on the table.

"You have a problem! You are abusive and you need to get help. I will never live with you again if you do not have a job and if you don't seek out treatment for your abusive behavior." I moved my daughter and me to a small apartment a few blocks from his house. Afterward, he and I attended a domestic abuse counseling program for six months. He seemed different and I agreed to try again. We moved to a beautiful two-bedroom apartment in a complex in St. Louis Park.

A mere two weeks later, his manipulative, controlling behavior kicked back in. He wanted me to quit my job. "If you didn't work so many hours, our relationship would be better. If you'd just pay more attention to me and Matilda, we could work it out. If you would just stay home and be a mom and housewife, this could work."

"I love my job and I spend plenty of time with you and Matilda," I argued. "In fact, I spend more time with our daughter than you do. I am not going to quit my job and I don't want to talk about this anymore."

He would then follow me from room to room, saying, "We need to talk about this now. If you were just as committed to us as you are to your job, we could work this out."

He would get louder and sterner, saying "Patti, we need to resolve this now!" This always led to me grabbing my purse and my daughter and leaving. I moved out in the third week into my own apartment in the same building.

After a year of therapy (this is the second separation we're talking about), I agreed to move in with him again. He convinced me to move to St. Paul (a place I definitely didn't want to live) and we rented a three-bedroom apartment (we now had separate bedrooms).

Within weeks, his controlling, compulsive behavior became more than I could tolerate, and I finally declared to our therapist that we were done. After four years, I had finally come to the conclusion that his behavior would never change. Recognizing the importance of my daughter having the example of a strong woman for a mother, rather than a woman who stayed to protect her daughter from the pain of a divorced family was a tipping point.

We lived together for three months after my declaration, agreeing to never be in the apartment together except during sleeping hours and I must say this was one of the most uncomfortable times of my life.

Many months earlier he had convinced me to quit my job for the sake of the marriage and I was now unemployed. He rented an apartment for me, and I found a temporary job.

It took over a year to complete the divorce proceedings. After a year of tears, screaming fights, sleepless nights, and frustration not to mention court dates, and meetings with lawyers, arbitrators, and mediators, I walked out of my lawyer's office with a divorce decree. I was stunned and numb as I made my way to my car, somehow finding myself in the huge parking garage. I ducked inside and the floodgates opened. I cried so hard I was gulping for air, my chest heaving up and down with no sign of stopping.

I was confused. I wanted the divorce and it was final. Why wasn't I elated? After the tsunami of tears subsided, I began to realize the outburst of emotions consisted of grief over the loss of a dream, the release of the tension I had been dealing with for twelve months, and the crushing realization that I still had to interact with the asshole I had divorced for the sake of my child. The relationship wasn't really over, just different.

Now I felt defeated. I had left a job I loved as a possible solution to our marriage and had been unemployed for a year. I had a five-year-old to raise and no idea what I wanted in my future except to be a great role model. I had not fought for sole custody and would receive financial support only if my ex-husband followed the 65/35 split of my daughter's expenses we had laid out in the divorce settlement. I had no savings and had been slapped with a $10,000 tax bill based on an IRS audit imposed upon us during the settlement. Things were a bit bleak, to say the least.

I was at a crossroads and needed to invent a new dream/future.

When facing this difficult and final decision to divorce my husband, I had to rely on my inner knowing and I had to take a stand for my future, our daughter's future, and my husband's future. It was apparent to my daughter, Matilda, at only eight years old that we could never get along when she exclaimed to me, "I don't know how you and Dad could ever live together!"

I had to have the courage to be the ONE who declared how the future will look. I *knew* that our daughter would grow up stronger with a mother who stood up for herself and that my husband would have a better life as well. If you are dealing with a difficult situation, trust your inner knowing and do the hard thing. That self-trust will pay off in the end.

CHAPTER 9

A New Life Emerges

"Optimism is the faith that leads to achievement."

Helen Keller

Now that I was divorced, what was I going to do with my life? All I knew was that I wanted to role model a powerful, successful woman for my daughter. I had not worked for over a year, and I needed a job, fast.

I jumped into action, applied at a temp agency, and secured a position working as the administrative assistant for the manager of an IT Division in a huge hospital system. The job paid so little, I could barely make ends meet, yet the work was much easier than in my past position. I worked hard and did more than was expected. I also was confident the boss was impressed and wanted me around, so one day I set up a meeting with him to explain my situation.

"I enjoy working for you, but I cannot live on the wage I am being paid. Unless you can increase that, I will sadly have to leave."

"How much do you want?" he answered.

I hadn't anticipated this question and replied, "Five dollars more per hour."

"I don't want to lose you, so I'll create a new position for you and pay you what you need," he responded.

I couldn't believe it. I was beyond ecstatic and I learned that I might as well ask for what I want or need because I just might get it. By the way, a few months later I asked for another raise when I realized how much he was paying others who did exactly what I was doing. He increased my pay another five dollars an hour. This was not my dream job, by any means, but it turned out to be a steppingstone to fulfilling my dreams.

Once I settled into my new job and life as a single mother, I started to design new dreams for my future. I wanted to buy my own home, find a healthy partner, and work in a job or career I loved and paid decent money. I have to tell you that over the next few years, each of these dreams came to fruition and more.

This began with buying a home. I was forty-five years old and had never owned my own home – something I now dearly desired. In 1997 it was a sellers' market in Minneapolis. Even though my income was on the lower side, I decided to explore the possibilities of homeownership. I found a mortgage broker who was able to approve up to $99,000 in mortgage funding for me. Now, that limited my choices, but I had a wonderful time searching every part of Minneapolis/St. Paul area and its suburbs.

I made twelve offers and I was outbid on most of them until one day I looked at a lovely, small, three-bedroom home built in the 1900s with a nine-foot vaulted ceiling. It was situated one block from a gorgeous, double-wide parkway and perfect for my daughter and me.

I was let go from my job two weeks before the closing, but I didn't tell anyone and everything went through easily. I was overjoyed! We had a home, and I was successful. A few years later, I bought over one million dollars in real estate. I still own that home today.

I secured another job quickly doing inside sales (something I am good at but don't love). Although I wasn't actively looking for a romantic partner, I was leading a seminar series and had been assigned a coach who lived in North Carolina. As the twelve weeks of the seminar progressed, I noticed that I had a crush on the gentleman.

I didn't give much credence to my feelings given that he was:

1) going through a divorce,
2) eight years younger,
3) lived in North Carolina, and
4) too good-looking (He used to be a football player.)

"I have this crush on my seminar coach," I shared with a friend one day.

"What are you going to do about it?" she said.

"Nothing, I don't want to ruin the relationship."

"That's silly," she said. "If you don't say anything to him, he won't know, and you could lose out on an amazing opportunity."

She was a very persuasive person and I ended up agreeing to converse with him about my feelings on our next call. A week later, after talking about the seminar I was leading, I screwed up enough courage. My heart pounded out of my chest, but I told him I had something I needed to tell him, but that I was worried it might mess up our relationship.

"But Sue said I had to tell you...I have a huge crush on you and," I was about to babble on, but he jumped into the conversation.

"Let me stop you right there, I feel the same way about you."

I started jumping for joy in my mind until, in the next breath he said, "But I don't want to do anything about it right now while I am going through this divorce."

My body deflated like a balloon that had been popped. The problem was that in the state of North Carolina you cannot even file for divorce for a year after you declare your intentions.

"I understand and thank you," I hung up, bewildered.

Should I just accept this, or could I alter his feelings somehow? All of a sudden, a thought hit me and I said to myself, I'm going to pick out four men I admire, tell them about this conversation and ask them what they recommend.

As I proceeded to ask this question to each of them, they each independently responded with a version of, "Don't listen to him, just tell him what to do!"

I was very encouraged by this and the next time we spoke I said to him, "I understand your reticence and I request you give it up and come visit me for Memorial Day Weekend."

"OK," he excitedly responded. It was as easy as that. He visited my daughter and me six weeks later and we have been together now for twenty-one years.

Within two years of connecting, he moved to Minnesota. One year later we were married.

Now was the time to find some work that I loved! I was bored to death in sales and one day I opened the newspaper to a one-page advertisement on becoming a Personal Life Coach. I was very excited by this prospect, as I had been a teacher and coach in all the jobs I loved. I attended an introductory meeting a few nights later, where I signed up for the training. I was trained and certified in six months and my husband told me to quit my job and hang out my shingle. I began to network madly and successfully secured twenty-five clients in my first year.

After divorcing Matilda's father, I was able to invent a new life for myself. First, I got a job so that I wouldn't be dependent on my ex-husband. I didn't know where or how that job would lead me to a fulfilling future, but I kept putting one foot in front of the other and creating what I wanted. I knew I wanted a home for my daughter and so I took the steps to make that happen.

I didn't know I wanted another relationship, but the right person came along, and I trusted myself and went for it. I knew I needed to do work that inspired and nurtured me and when I saw an opportunity, I seized it.

CHAPTER 10

A Child of Divorce

"Learn from the mistakes of others. You can't live long enough to make them all yourself." -
Eleanor Roosevelt

By the time my daughter turned six, I had been divorced, found my great man, purchased a home, and was on the way to my ideal career. However, co-parenting a child with a man you dislike and don't trust has its challenges.

I had opted for joint custody – something I regretted later – and had to share my daughter in a fifty-fifty split. My ex-husband was a stickler about this and counted the time down to the seconds. Giving my daughter over to him each week was gut-wrenching. She would stretch her arms out and hold onto the sides of his open car door, screaming and crying that she didn't want to go. He would physically force her into the car. I would watch in horror, go back into my apartment, and cry my eyes out. I prayed this would not scar her for a lifetime.

One stroke of luck came as a result of my ex-husband's controlling nature. Before she was born, he demanded that the only school she could attend was the Waldorf Private School. I looked it up and it seemed like a lovely place, so I said, "OK if you want to pay for a private school, it's fine with me."

Waldorf is a unique school where the child's imagination is more important than how early they learn to read. Teachers stay with their students for eight years. They learn through art, movement, drama, singing, playing the violin, and writing their own textbooks.

My daughter was in kindergarten when I got divorced and her teacher, Keri, was another angel in our lives. Keri supported Matilda as a wonderful grandmother would. I remember the first incident with my ex-husband was related to the number of days he took her during the week.

We met with Keri to discuss what she thought would work best for Matilda. Dwight (my ex-husband) had talked with a psychiatrist buddy of his and declared that "Patti has an unhealthy attachment to her daughter."

This really angered me and I experienced textbook blind rage. I felt my entire body erupt and I began to scream at him, "You are a fucking idiot! It's not my fault your daughter would rather spend time with me and not you. I am looking out for her welfare, not being attached."

Keri helped me to calm down, although I remember nothing more about the conversation. I left that day, shaking. I had never expressed myself in that way before and it felt unsafe. I imagine I would have liked to rage at my father that way many times, but never dared. Surprisingly, a few days later, Dwight agreed to the new schedule I had proposed. Something had gotten through!

Matilda loved her school. It provided a community apart from her two families – her father had become a born-again Christian and married a woman from his church. My husband and I were as liberal as you could get. (He's a non-practicing Jew, and I am an agnostic.)

One of my values as a parent was to allow my child to try on different ways of thinking and believing, challenge her about them, and then allow her to make her own decision. However, I will say that allowing her to try Christianity – especially the type taught at Dwight's mega-church – was difficult to maneuver.

When she was halfway through second grade, Dwight announced that she could no longer attend the Waldorf School because it was too humanistic, and this did not fit with their values.

Well, the divorce decree stated that she would attend Waldorf through the 8th grade, but we chose not to rub this in his face. Instead, my husband and I, along with Dwight and his wife, went to counseling together for six months to resolve this issue. We met a child psychologist, Deb, when Matilda was four years old. She was another angel in our lives. Often, our conversation was downright laughable – like the time that Nancy, Matilda's stepmother suggested we homeschool Matilda and she would be her teacher. (This from a woman who said her daughter could not swim in the pool while she was on her period.)

"Wouldn't you rather she was being taught by someone you know?" she argued.

"No, would you have wanted your girls to be homeschooled by me?" I countered.

We agreed to visit all the other possible school opportunities available. The only other school I would have considered was a public arts school, but Matilda couldn't start there until fourth grade.

"Over my dead body will she go anywhere but Waldorf," my current husband declared. So, we patiently went through the counseling process so that Dwight and Nancy could see it made no sense for her to leave Waldorf – and they eventually got it.

We visited the Maranatha Christian School – his top choice other than homeschooling – where the kids walk down the hall with their hands in the air. Way too creepy for me! We visited a Montessori school that no one liked. In the end, my husband and I, along with Deb, convinced them that the best option for Matilda's stability and health was to keep her with the community she loved.

Things went fairly smoothly until we had to transition Matilda to high school. Dwight saw this as a chance to get his way and have her attend the school of his choice. I got around this by giving her a choice. I told her we would visit every potential high school and she could decide.

I was rooting for the Arts High School, but it was too small, and didn't have the real high school experience. We lived within blocks of one of the best public high schools in the area, but it felt too big. She considered the Christian school affiliated with her dad's church, but it seemed too suppressive. She had attended Dwight's church every other Sunday until about the age of twelve when she decided they couldn't give her any good answers. She wanted to know why good people like me and her stepdad would go to hell if they weren't saved. This made no sense to her.

Finally, we visited the private Catholic school near us, and she fell in love. Not because of the faith aspect, but because they had a competitive, award-winning, show choir team performing all night long and she wanted to participate in that. Everyone agreed, although my husband hated the idea of paying for religious education. It turned out to be a wonderful environment for her. Just the right size and her participation in show choir gave her a great group of new friends.

Another big hurdle came when she turned fourteen. Dwight had a tendency to overreact to people who didn't treat him the way he wanted. I remember several frightening experiences as his wife.

For instance, he once slammed on the brakes of his car on the ramp of the freeway so the person behind us would hit us. (He had a large ball joint on the back and knew his car would not be hurt but theirs would.) I don't know what that poor driver had done to anger him. He often purposefully swam into someone in the pool lap lane because he had been angry at them for some reason. Dwight also screamed at people if they got to a parking spot before him. And, he was kicked out of a movie theater for life after he grabbed the ticket taker by the arm and threatened her.

One day when Matilda's father picked her up after school, she asked to bring her friend, Annalise, home with them. Dwight didn't like it when plans changed, and he was probably upset that she didn't just want to spend time with him. He begrudgingly accepted. He and Matilda started to have an argument in the car and by the time they arrived at his house, she and Annalise ran to the basement room and blocked the door. Typical behavior for teenagers. Well, he was so angry that he stormed down the steps, forced the door open, and shoved Annalise across the room.

I received a phone call from Matilda who sounded as though she'd been crying, "Mom, can I come home?"

"Of course. Did something happen?"

"Yes, and I'll tell you about it when I get there," she sniffed.

She arrived with a jumbo, black trash bag with everything she'd ever taken to his home and told me what had happened.

"Do I have to go back over there?"

"No, let him take us to court if he doesn't like it," I replied.

A few days later she informed him of her decision and told him she did not want him to text her, email her or call her. She said he could write letters and to his credit, he wrote her a letter every two weeks. A year later, after she had her driver's license, she was able to visit him weekly and a few years later, she was able to spend the night again. As an adult, she has a very good relationship with him.

Probably the scariest hurdle was when she turned fifteen. In his church, they encouraged a purity weekend. This was supposed to be a time when a mother takes her daughter, or a father takes his son, somewhere for the weekend. The time is centered around a curriculum to discuss puberty, set sexual boundaries, and sign a pledge to stay pure until marriage. Not only did I object to the content, but I also objected to him taking her to a remote part of the North Shore of Minnesota to a remote cabin where she would have no internet or access to her friends and me.

Everyone I mentioned this to told me I had to stop her from going. I wasn't sure what to do, but I screwed up my courage (I hadn't spoken to him in years) and called him.

My husband was on the other line, listening in and texting me as the conversation ensued. I expressed my concerns and Dwight refuted everyone. I grew more anxious by the minute, not knowing what else to say. Then he brought up my relationship with my father and once again, I experienced that blind rage. I screamed at him until I had nothing else to say and hung up. I had a splitting headache, and I didn't know if it made any difference, but guess what? The next day he sent me an email saying he could do the curriculum from home on a weekly basis.

"Hallelujah!"

The funny thing is, he asked me to do the unit on sex and his whole plan backfired. She and I got to have deep discussions where I would ask, "What do you think about that? – whatever the tape was espousing – and she ended up creating her own boundaries aside from religious dogma. This program wanted her to believe holding hands was an impure action, which she knew was ridiculous. I also requested she not sign a purity pledge, and she was in total agreement.

Raising children is challenging enough in a congruent, loving family. However, fifty percent or more households are raising children of divorce. In addition, even if you don't have children, this chapter is about the challenges of being related to others. What pulled me through these times was knowing what was important to me and what I valued. This allowed me to be strong, express anger when appropriate, and not back down. It was a tough game, but my daughter, Matilda, grew up to be one of the most amazing, smart, funny, creative people I know. She is a natural with people and everyone who meets her, loves her.

Her father mellowed as he aged, and they are very close today.

CHAPTER 11

Devastating Illness

"It's not the absence of fear, it's overcoming it.
Sometimes you've got to blast through
and have faith."

Emma Watson

The year I turned sixty was an exciting year. I was poised to enter this new decade with enthusiasm for everything I intended and created for it. Throughout the year, I kept declaring to my friends that sixty was going to be my best year yet. Not only was my business very successful that year but I found some amazing new friends and I was on top of the world. I had planned a big birthday party and my siblings planned to fly to Minnesota in December to celebrate with me.

However, in early December, I noticed strange bruising that had no reason to be there, and my mucus became bloody. After researching these symptoms on the internet, I decided I had a virus and the blood in my nose was a function of the dry winter heat.

Soon after, I woke up with two large, black sores on my tongue. I rushed to urgent care, but they had no idea what they were. They, too, decided it must be a virus.

Each day in December a new bruise appeared. I can't say I felt very happy at my December 20th birthday bash. I took off the next day for our annual Christmas trip to Cancun, but I never put on a bathing suit. I had about fifty bruises up and down my legs and arms, and many other places that won't be named. I felt like a hammer was smashing into the side of my head and constantly uttered, *Ouch!* every fifteen minutes or so.

When I returned home, I went to see my primary care doctor. She was also stumped and still thought I had a virus. She ordered some blood tests and sent me on my way, but within the hour she called, "You should drive immediately to the emergency room because the blood tests show your platelets are only at four-thousand and you could nick your esophagus and bleed to death!"

My breath caught in my throat, and I couldn't believe what I heard. I grabbed my husband and we zoomed to the hospital, where I was admitted immediately, and the injections and testing began. After having X-rays to determine a brain bleed, massive doses of cortisone, IVs of platelets (which induced vomiting), and many blood tests, I was diagnosed with a condition called ITP (Idiopathic thrombocytopenic purpura), an autoimmune deficiency where the body makes platelets but kills them off. This is a very rare blood disease that affects 200,000 people globally.

After four days in the hospital getting more tests and IVs with hemoglobin, I was discharged with a platelet count of 12,000. We drove home and I went straight to the bedroom and wept. My world had turned upside down. I didn't know how to act, what to do or not do, or what the future was going to look like.

For the first three months, I took 100 mg of prednisone each day. I was wired, exhausted, and hungry all the time. Everywhere I went I ran into something and ended up with the largest, ugliest bruises I had ever seen. It was freaky, to say the least. I saw my hematologist every week and prayed that my platelets had gone up but each week the nurse would hand me a report with the words CRITICAL written on the top.

My platelet levels had dropped back to four thousand by the Friday after I left the hospital, and even dropped to zero at one point.

As the weeks passed, it felt as though all the hope I had mustered drained from me until my plans for my birthday celebration completely evaporated. I was not focusing on my business. Instead, I felt burdened by what it meant to live with this threatening disease for the rest of my life. I sought a second opinion at the University of Minnesota and was overwhelmed by the hematologist's declaration that I was a ticking time bomb and could have a brain bleed at any moment.

I decided to stick with my original doctor, who was not such an alarmist. For fear of being injured, I was driving as little as possible, cooking with special gloves, and wearing special things on my shoes so as not to slip on the ice. My life was altered in ways I could never have imagined. I felt defeated.

There came a point where I had to revive myself and my life. I was depressed, gaining weight, and getting nothing accomplished. My platelets were not changing for the better, no matter what medications I took.

Consequently, and after researching and talking with others dealing with the disease, I made the radical choice to go off all my medication and simply live with the risk. I began to come out of my depression and will always remember the day that Roger Ebert died. He was a famous movie critic who had lived with cancer of the thyroid and salivary glands that left him unable to speak for many years. I had a lot of respect for him.

Friends were posting famous quotes from him on Facebook. One that hit me especially hard was, "To make others less happy is a crime. To make ourselves unhappy is where all crime starts. We must try to contribute joy to the world. That is true no matter what our problems, our health, our circumstances. We must try. I didn't always know this and am happy I lived long enough to find it out."

That day I said to myself, "Get off your butt and start contributing what you have to offer in the world." I called my friend, Marny, set up a meeting where she helped me begin to restructure my business. We met, created, and held each other to account for two years. As I write this seven years later, my platelets hovered between five and twelve thousand. I have been attacked by a dog, fallen head/face-first into concrete, banged into countless things, and cut myself with no major consequences.

I don't know why, but I don't have spontaneous bruising, tongue sores, bloody snot, or much of any symptoms anymore. But more importantly, I am having an amazing life in my 60s. I restructured my business so that I don't have to stand for hours or leave my house much. I am happier with my work than I have ever been!

When something shocking, threatening and unexpected occurs, our tendency is to withdraw and retreat until we can make sense of it and reset our lives. Unfortunately, we can get frozen and stay stuck for the rest of our lives. During the six-month period that I was adjusting, I researched my condition and found groups online of people who dealt with the same situation. This empowered me and allowed me to make conscious choices about how to live my life going forward. Again, I used the support of the community and people in my life, declared what I wanted for my life, and took the necessary action to fulfill my hopes and dreams.

CHAPTER 12

A Final Move

*"I learned a long time ago that there is
something worse than missing the goal, and
that's not pulling the trigger."*

Mia Hamm

After being diagnosed with ITP, I convinced my husband to move to Florida. I remember when he proposed and I said, "I'll only marry you if you agree to move to Florida or somewhere warm when the time is right."

He said, "I can do that."

I hated the cold weather in Minnesota, and I was trapped with joint custody raising my daughter. I knew, however, that I did not want to grow old there and would leave when it felt right to do so. Since my daughter had been at college for two years and I now had a disease where it was especially important that I not slip on the ice and hit my head, I decided that the time was right to move.

My husband was a bit resistant when the actual move began to manifest as he had grown to love Minnesota. But he remembered his agreement and we scheduled a trip to find our new home in or near my hometown of Clearwater, Florida.

We flew down the last week of January, a good time to leave Minnesota, and looked at fifty houses over five days, none of which seemed to meet our standards. That is until the last house of the last day. I had added four new homes to our search the night before and as soon as we walked up the walkway to this unique pink house on a corner lot with floor to ceiling windows in the front and the back, we looked at each other and he exclaimed, "I'm liking this one."

As we continued through the house each room had a new and interesting quality. The floors were original wood, the kitchen was large and open, the master suites on either side of the house had their own baths, the bathrooms were covered with the original, colored tile we loved, the back porch was hand-painted with Floridian flowers and birds, and the fully enclosed back yard had a pool, Jacuzzi, and outdoor shower.

My husband said, "We should make an offer!" and I jumped for joy.

I could not go back to Minnesota without a home in Florida. We closed on the house and moved in on March 18th of the same year. The temperature that day was -11 in Minnesota and 75 in Florida and at that point, my husband said, "I think we made the right decision!"

Now that I lived somewhere I loved, I needed to redesign the work I was doing so that I loved it, too. I needed to deal with physical restrictions due to my blood disease that manifested in low energy. Working exclusively from home minimized the likelihood of catching colds and flu easily, allowing me the comfort of a healthy, safe environment.

I am a people person. I get energy from being with people, so working at home alone often left me feeling lonely and unmotivated. I needed to see and interact with others every day, several times a day.

I was working with a business coach at the time, and she suggested I open a community where I could support others like me. Solopreneurs who work at home alone and struggle with loneliness and a lack of support and accountability. This was a brilliant idea. I began inviting everyone I knew from Minnesota, California, and Florida to participate and I quickly grew my community to fifty participants.

I was able to design the community so that all of our interactions took place online via Zoom and email. I had weekly coaching groups, daily co-working sessions, weekly planning sessions, and monthly special interest events. I didn't start any programs before 10:00 and was easily done every day by 3:00. It was glorious.

I couldn't wait to see my people every day, and the aspects of the community were making a major difference for my clients. Over the eight years, I have been running the community. The way it's organized has changed but the impact remains the same.

By staying true to my sense that I wanted to continue to contribute and needed to create something that would both work for me and my clients, I was able to develop a business that works all the way around.

A theme you may have noticed running through this book is how important it is to find the support you need. Without a coach, I probably would not have come up with this idea and have had the confidence to implement it. If you have an interest in joining us, hop on over to www.sagethink.com. I run weekly, affordable support groups and they could be the beginning of a change for you. By the way, they are not just for solopreneurs.

CHAPTER 13

The "C" Word

"If you don't like the road you're walking, start paving another one."

Dolly Parton

I picked up the phone and the person on the other end said, "Hi, this is Mary from the Susan G Komen Breast Center. We would like you to come in for an ultrasound as there is a suspicious shadow on your mammogram."

I was not overly worried as I had gotten the same phone call a year earlier and I figured that my large, fibrous breasts were the problem, so I made the appointment. After the ultrasound was completed and I lay on the table with my breast exposed, the radiologist arrived and declared to tell me I had a tumor which he was sure was cancerous.

We needed to do a biopsy, but given that my platelets were low, he needed to do some research before scheduling it. He asked who my hematologist was. I didn't have one but agreed to find someone immediately to determine if and how my platelets could be increased.

I felt a bit numb leaving the clinic and wondered why he said the tumor was cancerous before doing the biopsy. I wasn't too freaked out, as my sister had gone through the exact situation the year before with no complications. She was cancer-free. I figured I would simply get a lumpectomy, undergo radiation, and take chemo drugs (something I dreaded).

I found a hematologist who convinced me to try Rituxan (a four-week IV treatment) that often brings platelets back to normal. As I took this treatment, I kept wondering why, after the cancer is removed, one must have radiation and chemo. I started researching and what I discovered changed the course of my life.

I learned that generally cancers grow for two to seven years before being detected and when you remove cancer surgically, it wants to grow back quickly, thus requiring radiation and chemo to arrest the growth.

I also learned that cancer loves sugar and our processed, American diets feed the growth of cancer and weaken our immune systems. You see, a strong immune system is constantly destroying cancer that is growing. I learned that many people are curing their cancer by changing their lifestyles and eating a plant-based diet. They detox their bodies, the air about them, and the water in their environment. Many also reconnect to deep spiritual beliefs. I learned that cancer can be a gift!

After a failed attempt at raising my platelets, I was given a platelet transfusion. The biopsy revealed a small, slow-growing tumor. I then had an MRI, which revealed that the tumor had not spread to my lymph nodes. I was scheduled for surgery a week later but called it off.

I was terrified of being put under anesthesia and of being cut open, given my platelet situation. I wanted to learn more about my alternatives. The sad part of all this is, that the medical community does not make available any alternative practices.

For eighteen months I ate a sugar-free, plant-based diet, meditated, and visualized a healthy me every day as I lay in my infrared sauna. I had lymphatic drainage massages monthly, juiced four pounds of carrots, beets, celery, ginger, and turmeric daily, took prescribed supplements, and worked on de-stressing my life.

Then COVID-19 hit, and I began to feel I needed to do something more proactive. I knew I needed support around this, so I hired a cancer coach – a gentleman who cured Stage IV, untreatable cancer through natural means.

He suggested I get a second opinion through the research-based National Cancer Institute. I accepted his request. After extensive scans and biopsies, I learned that cancer had grown and spread to my lymph nodes but had not metastasized. The surgeon – someone who made me feel extremely comfortable – said he thought we could pop the tumors out and I'd be done.

Although I had decided to have the operation, I was denied the surgery because of my platelet count. This brought on a whole new conundrum. I decided I had better look for a hematologist I felt understood me and work with him to determine if and how we might raise my platelets should I ever need surgery. I connected with a lovely man and underwent four days of a steroids, dexamethasone, and two grueling days of IVs filled with gammagard – a hemoglobin product. I had experienced both of these interventions eight years earlier to no avail. However, this time my platelets rose to 175,000. Now I could safely have the surgery.

I had the surgery which was much more extensive than I anticipated. I must say I was shocked when I woke to find two very bruised breasts (I had approved having the left breast match the right), as well as a large incision under my right arm. I didn't get clarity on what this would entail before the surgery, and it took over three months to heal and get full motion in my right arm. I am undergoing IV treatment every three weeks for one year and six weeks of radiation in the hopes of keeping the cancer at bay.

In the end, I wish I had chosen surgery three years prior as it would have been less invasive. However, dwelling in woulda, shoulda, coulda is never of any use. For whatever reason, I needed the time to think, wonder and change in order to be ready to resolve my cancer.

I thought after the surgery, I would forget about cancer and I realized, the potential return is a constant companion. I see however that I can interpret this as something negative or use it to remind myself of how precious each moment of my life is and to strengthen my peaceful relationship to my impending death now or in the future.

I view cancer as a wake-up call. I have used it to transform many areas of my life, including my diet, my stress levels, my environment, my connection with others, and my relationship to my divine self. I do not want to fight with it. I like to dance with it and use it to improve my life. It could kill me but so could many other things. It has been a journey and an adventure. I am grateful for the changes it has brought to my life.

Sometimes we make choices based on the information we have at the time. Later we make different choices based on different information. This is a normal, natural process and one to be honored. The universe is giving us what we need when we need it. Just as my old friend, Phil, said to me so many years ago, "Trust that when you need something, it will be provided."

CHAPTER 14

An Exciting Adventure

"I was exhilarated by the new realization that I could change the character of my life by changing my beliefs. I was instantly energized because I realized that there was a science-based path that would take me from my job as a perennial "victim" 'to my new position as '"co-creator" of my destiny."

Bruce H. Lipton Ph.D.

One morning I was attending a networking event and a woman, Judy, stood up and said, "I help people rewrite limiting beliefs on a subconscious level."

"Hmm," I thought, "that sounds interesting."

I set up a lunch meeting with her and the more she talked, the more interested I became. I scheduled time with Judy to experience the process she had described to me. In our meeting, the first thing she asked me to do was list what areas of my life I wanted to work on – areas where I felt restricted or stuck.

I explained that after I was diagnosed with all of my health issues, I noticed that I was often battling a loud, internal conversation that went like this:

"If you had just..., you'd be making more money. If you had just..., you'd be healthier. If you had just..., you could have been ..., If you had just..., you'd be thinner and in better shape."

Along with this, my inner dialogue would try to convince me that I was now too old to make any of my dreams come true. It was too late. I should just retire.

I was enjoying running my business, but I wasn't making enough money and didn't see how I ever could. This made me feel like a failure. My husband was charging thousands for his services, while I couldn't get myself to ask for what I felt I was worth.

"First, that was the most fascinating thing I have experienced in years, and second, the world looks and feels different," was how I explained to my husband what shifted for me in that meeting with Judy.

I went on with my life as usual and a few weeks later, I realized that my woulda, shoulda, coulda conversations had disappeared. I felt free and present and was enjoying my life. I decided to send my daughter and my husband for sessions.

My daughter has suffered most of her life with extreme anxiety. She would call me several times a week, revved up, frustrated, and angry, crying, screaming, and sometimes hitting herself. I could assuage her but that made her dependent on me. After doing two sessions with a facilitator, she never calls me in that state. Ever.

My husband used the session to resolve his anxiety around his work and credits it to his easy loss of fifty pounds he struggled with for years.

I was fascinated and decided to train in this discipline called PSYCH-K® so that I could bring it to my clients. I spent six months in 2019 studying and learning to become a facilitator. PSYCH-K® is a process by which you access the subconscious mind in order to rewrite limiting beliefs. As a result, all resistance to accomplishing what you want falls away and you find yourself with new and exciting results.

I have been bringing this new skill to my clients since March 2019 and the results have been phenomenal. My business has morphed as a result and in addition to offering my weekly support groups, I now spend most of my days facilitating PSYCH-K® sessions. In my late sixties, everything I have ever done and learned in my life has come together and the work I am doing now is more fulfilling than I ever imagined. By the way, my block around charging for my services has disappeared and for the first time, I am making a six-figure income with ease.

The most important trait to honor in your life is to stay open to learning new things. No matter what age you are or what trials and tribulations you have endured, it is never too late to reinvent yourself and your life. The second half of this book gives you techniques and processes that will support you as you think and reassess who you are at any point. Please use them over and over as your life changes with the tides.

Section 2

Getting Free

"Above all, be the heroine of your life,
not the victim."

Nora Ephron

If you are reading this book, I know that you are in the middle of some type of life transition and your intuition, inner knowing, or trust in your higher power has led you to this work. I invite you to trust the process I am laying before you and begin to envision and create the next exciting phase of your life.

It's time to reinvent your life by taking action today. You can never go back but you can always move forward.

I have laid out a step-by-step plan for you to follow. You can work the plan in the order it is laid out, or you can pick and choose what feels right.

If you would like more personalized assistance or support, please visit my website at www.sagethink.com and sign up for a complimentary session with me.

FOCUS 1

Clarity, Vision and Values

*"Make the most of yourself by fanning the tiny,
inner sparks of possibility into flames of
achievement."*

Golda Meir

Perhaps the most critical step in designing and inventing what's next in your life is getting CLARITY regarding what you want. After my daughter moved away to go to college, I began to envision how I wanted the rest of my life to look, what I wanted to be doing, where I wanted to live, etc.

One of the best ways to get clarity is to use your imagination to create your IDEAL VISION.

***VISION** is defined as the act or power of
anticipating that which will or may come to be:
a vivid, imaginative conception or anticipation.*

82

As you can see by the definition, a vision allows you to play and pretend, to suspend what you think you can or can't do, and make up an IDEAL world. If you were six years old this would be an exciting task, so take yourself back to a younger self and let it rip.

You might feel afraid that you can't achieve what you imagine. Keep letting go of whether you know how to do something or have the time, money, or energy, and surrender to your imagination. Fear is kind of SHORT-SIGHTEDNESS and often we sell ourselves short by relating what we can do in our future to what we have or haven't been able to do in our past.

CLARITY is defined as clearness or lucidity as to perception or understanding; freedom from indistinctness or ambiguity.

VALUE is defined as a principle, standard, or quality considered worthwhile or desirable.

Getting clear on your VALUES AND VISION is the first step on your way to developing a new life. The exercises outlined below will help you begin to form that VISION and once you have that vision, you will be able to map out a plan. Do not worry about how to execute that plan, instead let it inspire you. The remaining exercises are designed to assist you with this process.

Let your imagination soar as you engage in the following exercises. You will find worksheets to use for all exercises on my website at www.sagethink.com.

"Make your vision so clear that you're fears become irrelevant."

Anonymous

Getting Free Exercises

Step 1: Values Clarification.

"Values are who we are, not who we want to be. Values represent our unique and individual essence, our ultimate and most fulfilling form of expressing and relating. They serve as a compass pointing out what it means to be true to oneself. When we honor our values on a regular and consistent basis life is good, life is fulfilling." Laura Whitworth, Co-Active Coaching.

The Laura Whitworth Values-Based Decision Matrix

Brainstorm a list of your values and write them below. On the next page, rank your top ten values in order of priority on the VALUES WORKSHEET

Next, score your sense of satisfaction – the degree to which you are honoring each value – using a scale of 0 to 10.

Sample Values List
- Humor Participation Accomplishment Adventure
- Directness Performance Full Self-Expression Beauty
- Partnership Collaboration Integrity Lack of Pretense
- Service Personal Power Orderliness Authenticity
- Service Community Forward the Action Risk Taking
- Contribution Freedom to Choose Creativity Tradition
- Excellence Connectedness Honesty Peace
- Free Spirit Acknowledgment Independence To Be Known
- Focus Comradeship Success Elegance

- Romance Lightness Nurturing Growth
- Recognition Spirituality Accuracy Vitality
- Harmony Empowerment Joy Trust

Values Worksheet

Value (by Priority)	Level of Satisfaction (0 to 10)
1.	
2.	
3.	
4.	
5.	
6.	
7.	
8.	
9.	
10.	

Step 2:

List one-hundred things you want to do, be, or have in the next ten years, imagine you have no restrictions around money, time, or energy. See if you can keep going until you get to one hundred, as often amazing things open up as you work through this. Be as specific as you can and list every country or city you want to visit, the title of every book you want to read, etc.

The 100 Things List

100.

99.

98.

97

96.

95.

94.

93.

92.

91.

90.

89.

88.

87.

86.

85.

84.

83.

82.

81.

80.

79.

78.

77.

76.

75.

74.

73.

72.

71.

70.

69.

68.

67.

66.

65.

64.

63.

62.

61.

60.

59.

58.

57.

56.

55.

54.

53.

52.	26.
51.	25.
50.	24.
49.	23.
48.	22.
47.	21.
46.	20.
45.	19.
44.	18.
43.	17.
42.	16.
41.	15.
40.	14.
39.	13.
38.	12.
37.	11.
36.	10.
35.	9.
34.	8.
33.	7.
32.	6.
31.	5.
30.	4.
29.	3.
28.	2.
27.	1.

Step 3: My 10 Years from Now Letter

Write a letter to someone as though it was ten years from now describing what has happened in your life as though it has already happened. (See appendix A for examples.)

Step 4: Listen to *Envisioning Your Future*, a recording at www.sagethink.com, and journal what you see, hear or feel.

How Christina Overcame a Difficult Situation by Standing for What Was Important to Her

From the age of seven to thirteen, I was sexually abused by my grandfather. My father is originally from Costa Rica and his parents would send airfare for me to come visit them, as well as the extended family every summer. I looked forward to it every year, except for the nights when my grandfather would come into my bed, wake me up, and perform oral sex on me. I remember that I would pretend to be asleep and luckily, he never tried to penetrate me. This happened every summer, randomly, and was a huge dark secret I kept from everyone. I knew it was wrong, but I didn't know who to tell or how to tell them.

When I was thirteen, I had an epiphany. I got clarity about the situation and what I wanted to do about it and why. My little sister was two, plus a number of younger cousins had been born. Most of them lived in the area and I realized I thought I was taking it for the team. I came to believe my grandfather would probably start molesting them as well.

That summer I told my aunt about it and her reaction was matter of fact. This was confusing and disheartening. When I got home, I finally told my parents about what had happened, and they were very supportive of me. I was relieved they believed me and trusted that what I said was true. They confronted my grandparents and I didn't return to Costa Rica until I was twenty. This was sad because I missed my extended family and particularly my grandmother.

How did I heal from this trauma? My parents sent me to a psychologist who specialized in sexual trauma. I worked with her all through high school and it made all the difference in minimizing its ability to haunt me throughout my life. Therapy gave me a sense of peace around my experience. There have been challenges associated with it in my marriage of nearly thirty years, but we have successfully worked through them.

I realized that many people don't have parents who believe and support them. This was my father's father and my parents cut off all contact with my grandparents, had nothing to do with them. The greater extended family knew something must have happened. I found out later that somebody told my godparents and my godparents supposedly investigated. There was a little bit of a family rumor mill going on.

When my father's grandfather died and I went to the funeral with my fifteen-month-old son, I was confronted for the first time by a family member who didn't believe me. I was verbally assaulted by one of my cousins for decimating my grandfather's name. My aunt raised her four daughters to worship my grandfather. They didn't call him grandfather. They called him "Papa," as in "father."

With a calm demeanor, I defended myself and my character by plainly stating that I never talked about what had happened to me while in Costa Rica. I explained that I was purposefully quiet about it – all the while I was holding my fifteen-month-old (who had an ear infection). It was a bizarre experience. And an initiation of the soul by fire.

To stand up to that kind of emotional barrage was one of the most challenging times in my life. I had to keep standing up for my values with clarity and not back down. When I was confronted in that environment again, I could see how deep the tendrils of those roots go.

Often girls who are abused go one of two ways, angelic or promiscuous. And thankfully I didn't go either way. I was able to process my abuse and continue processing it. I think going through my freshman year of high school with counseling gave me the ability to be courageous.

I remember writing a poem and repeating it out loud to my entire English class. It was about the abuse and my anger around the situation, which was heavy to lay on a class of ninth-graders, but allowed me greater clarity regarding my values. I realized that I could always choose to be true to myself and continue to work on myself.

I spent a semester in Germany and continued to develop myself and learned to handle various situations: different cultures and different people. In my senior year of high school, I enrolled in a peer counseling class and developed leadership skills because of the counseling. It felt good to use my experience to help many others.

As a mom, business owner, and wife, clarity of values has guided me throughout my life and often given me the strength to confront difficult situations, to move through them and to the other side.

Cristina Eury, Acupuncturist who deals with chronic conditions and helps people prepare their mind and body for surgery with less pain and quick recovery. info@ancientflow.com

FOCUS 2

COURAGE

*"I choose to make the rest of my life
the best of my life."*

Louise Hay

Every major life transition includes FEAR. You have to find some level of COURAGE, TRUST, BELIEF AND FAITH to move forward into the next phase of your life. You could see this transformation in my stories of moving to Los Angeles with $80, choosing to divorce, and restarting my life after being diagnosed with a life-threatening illness.

The first way to combat fear is by understanding what drives your fear.

***FEAR is defined as a distressing emotion
aroused by impending danger, evil, pain, etc.,
whether the threat is real or imagined or
anticipation of the possibility that something
unpleasant will occur.***

As you can see by the definition, fear causes distress, dread, apprehension, and even panic – whether the threat is real or imagined. In the case of making a life change, most if not all of our fear is imagined; based on the projection that something unpleasant will or could occur. I know it took me five years to choose to divorce my ex-husband because I feared it would screw up my daughter's life and that I might not be able to support us on my own.

The opposite of fear is COURAGE. It took courage for me to take a stand with no evidence that my daughter would be better off if I divorced her father and that I could and would make a great life for her and I.

COURAGE is defined as the quality of mind or spirit that enables a person to face difficulty, danger, pain, etc., without fear; BRAVERY.

You will probably face fear initially, but it is possible to act in the face of the fear by bringing forth your bravery and taking powerful actions that move you forward. The interesting thing is that the opposite of courage is not fear, it is COWARDICE. I know you have the bravery and courage within you to stand up in the face of any adversity and move your life forward in a meaningful way.

No matter what life transition you are experiencing, FEAR of the UNKNOWN FUTURE is always a major factor. So how do you find the COURAGE to move forward and take the risks necessary to fulfill your dreams and goals?

Trust and Believe

The experience of FEAR, COURAGE, TRUST, or BELIEF stems from your belief system that exists in your conscious and/or subconscious. If you believe that life is scary, you will find that many things in your life seem scary.

Whereas, if you believe life is exciting you will find most of what you encounter to be exciting. Your beliefs give you your view of everything and you see through that filter. Therefore, by examining your limiting beliefs and developing empowering beliefs you will find the strength to move forward. In my story of moving to Los Angeles, I was afraid to make the trip for fear that I would fail. My friend helped me stay strong by suggesting I change the belief that I would fail to the empowering belief that what I needed would be there when I needed it.

By living in and generating that belief I have experienced over and over again in my life, that the universe provides me with what I need, who I need, etc., when I need it or them.

I have designed the following exercise that allows you to connect with your fears, see the limiting belief under them, create a new, empowering belief, and begin to take the step necessary to move forward into the next phase of your life.

Getting Free Exercise

Step 1:

Choose something you want to accomplish that feels scary or risky. (i.e. start dating again, request a raise, look for a new job, move, etc.)

Step 2:

Determine what belief or beliefs about your choice for step one make you feel scared. (i.e. all the good men are taken, I don't deserve a raise, the new job could be worse, I won't know anyone)

Step 3:

Make up a new belief or beliefs that make you feel happy, encouraged, and empowered. (i.e. there is an amazing man out there that can't wait to meet me, I am worth a massive raise, my new job will be amazing and further my career, I make new friends easily and effortlessly and can't wait for a new experience.)

Step 4:

Print your new belief out and read it several times a day. There is no guarantee about anything in life but operating from an empowering belief will always give you the COURAGE and STRENGTH to take the risks necessary to live an amazing life.

Step 5:

Imagining that you have no FEAR, brainstorm all possible actions you could take (you haven't committed to any of them) to accomplish this new goal.

Step 6:

Pick one to three of the actions above that you are willing to take and schedule them in your calendar. When you've taken those actions, pick one to three more. As the saying goes, "Rome wasn't built in a day." Taking small consistent action over time is the key to building the next phase of your life.

This is an exercise you can use over and over again to clarify your goals and design a powerful place to stand as you live them out.

How Nancy Found the Courage to Leave an Abusive Marriage

The dictionary defines courage as the ability to do something that frightens oneself. That courage might be facing your fears, trying something new, or speaking up when no one else will. Courage comes in all sizes, each one important to us in its unique way. On April 13th, 2011 at 10:22 p.m., I faced my biggest challenge in life and found the courage to face it, head-on!

For fourteen years I was married to someone who was supposed to be my partner for life. It started that way; he would shower me with gifts and expensive trips. Life was great and I was in love! We decided to elope and live in marital bliss. One month after we married, he moved me four hundred miles away from all of my family and friends and the only home I knew. He convinced me it was because he worked in this new city and it would be best for us to move.

It was quite an adjustment because I didn't have any friends in this new city and felt like I was completely starting over. I had my son from a previous marriage and my new husband insisted that I stay home to raise him. He reminded me often that "a woman's place was at home, taking care of babies and keeping the house." I thought he loved me so much, that I ignored the red flags that were right in front of me.

As the years passed, he became more and more controlling. He would remind me about my "role" quite often and would tell me that I was useless. He would often criticize me and tell me that I was dumb while reminding me that I could never function without him. After each ridicule or insult, he would laugh and tell me to stop being so sensitive. After all, he said he loved me and I believed him. I knew that his words were hurtful, but at least he wasn't hurting me physically.

That all changed the night he came home from a night of drinking with his friends. I was sleeping when he walked into the room and lay on top of me. I thought it was an intruder, so I tried pushing him off. Something inside him snapped, and he started to punch me. I was pushed off the bed as he continuously kicked me. I managed to get up and run outside the bedroom.

My goal was to get outside the house and run to a neighbor's house. As I reached for the doorknob, he grabbed me by the neck and pinned me to the wall while whispering to me that if I walked out the door, he would kill me. I not only feared for my life, but for our three children that were sleeping. I managed to calm him down and convinced him that he was tired and needed to go to bed. As he went to bed, I sat on the couch holding a knife in fear of being attacked again.

Our marriage went downhill after that night. The mental, verbal and physical abuse got worse every night. I lived in constant fear for my life. I knew that this was not the life that I deserved and my children deserved a better life, too. It took two years of planning, but I eventually found the courage to stand up to my abusive husband and say, "No more!". I had to heal from this toxic relationship and the best way I knew to do that was by empowering other women to find the courage to stand up to their abusers. That moment that you can do something that frightens you, is when you find the courage to conquer anything!

Nancy Gonzalez, Founder | Advocate | Speaker | Author
Mustard Seed Bags of Courage
http://www.mustardseedbagsofcourage.org,
mustardseedbagsofcourage@yahoo.com

Creativity

"We do not need magic to change the world, we carry all the power we need inside ourselves already: we have the power to imagine better."

J.K. Rowling

When our lives have been buzzing along in a certain rhythm and at an enjoyable pace and something comes along to interrupt that flow, we often have a feeling of being defeated.

You might find yourself saying, "Dang it, things were going so well and now I have to figure out how to make a change. I don't want this! I like things the way that they were."

Unfortunately, life is unpredictable, and we may have to deal with feeling defeated more than we like.

In my story, I needed a job and a place to live in Los Angeles. This left me with an enormous sense of DEFEAT, UNCERTAINTY, and FEAR. I was able to overcome these feelings through supportive RELATIONSHIPS and tapping into my CREATIVITY to discover a situation that was even more ideal than what I had lost.

*CREATIVITY is defined as the skill and
imagination to create new things, the ability to
form mental images of things that either are
not physically present or have never been
conceived or created by others.*

You might not feel creative, or you may think "I'm not a creative person." This is not true. You don't have to be artistic or have some identified talent to be creative. You simply need to practice thinking creatively.

The opposite of creativity is dullness or ordinariness.

Feelings of defeat often occur when you are forced to make a change. Examples of this are divorce, job loss, relocation, serious illness, or significant loss of a person or pet. There are two reactions you can have to defeat. You can either let it take you under and never recover, or you can bounce back and use the experience as a catalyst for success.

In my story about bouncing back after being diagnosed with a life-threatening blood disease, I was able to accept the situation, create a new life vision, and begin to re-generate my life.

The following exercise will assist you in letting the past go by appreciating it and allowing the future to unfold by bringing forth your CREATIVITY.

Getting Free Exercise

Step 1:

Identify the situation that has you feeling defeated. (Loss of a job, divorce, death of a loved one, relocation, illness, etc.)

Step 2: Answer the following questions:

What did you accomplish? (During the marriage – had a beautiful child, the job – bought a house, in the relationship – got clarity on what I want, from the illness – designed a new way of working, etc.)

What are you most proud of from that time?

Where did you fall short during that period? Will you let any regrets go?

What strengths did you develop during that time?

Who do you need to forgive (including yourself) to complete that period of your life and let it go? Can you forgive? Will you forgive?

Who can you acknowledge for supporting you during that period of your life? Will you acknowledge their support and encouragement?

What else needs to happen for you to release the past and move forward into the future?

You will know that this section of the process is done when you feel a release of energy, natural enthusiasm for creating "what's next," and are looking forward to being in action.

There may be places where you get stuck or stopped by emotions like anger, resentment, or other self-defeating feelings. And you may need to seek out support from a personal coach, therapist, pastor, rabbi, or another mentor. I encourage you to give yourself the gift of being supported. You are worth it!

Step 3:

Design a new future/declare what's next in a new area. I suggest you begin by creating this new reality by visualizing the outcome. Then, get to work on the manifestation of that vision.

If you lost your job, begin creating all the details of your next ideal job, if you lost your marriage, begin creating a fabulous single life or the next ideal mate, if your child moved on to adulthood, begin creating how you want to use your time and how you can keep contributing to others, and so forth. Create goals related to the new future you are designing. Use the following questions to guide you. What goals do I have for myself in this new area of my life?

What new skills do I need to develop to thrive in this new era of my life?

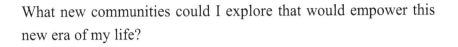

What new communities could I explore that would empower this new era of my life?

What new hobbies might I take on in this new era of my life?

What actions do I see to take now to move this new era of my life forward?

Step 4: Take the actions you identified above.

Action	Date by When?	Done
		☐
		☐
		☐
		☐
		☐
		☐
		☐
		☐
		☐
		☐
		☐
		☐

Feathers and Stones –
How Michele Used Creativity
to Regenerate Her Life

Prairie grasses and alfalfa grow tall by the end of July in Pocatello, Idaho. In the early morning hours, each blade will be painted with a delicate sheen of dew left by the cold nights. Even in the baking sun of the summer months, the high plains desert valley is refreshed by cool temperatures. It always seemed to me that the moment the sun hit the land, the unique perfume of sagebrush blended with the spice of the Russian Olive Trees was released.

The summer of 1975 I would search my dresser drawers for my favorite pink seersucker shorts and halter top edged in white lace, throw on a pair of sneakers, run a comb through my Dorothy Hamill haircut, gulp down a bowl of Trix saturated in cold, crisp Meadowgold milk and dash outside.

In our one-acre pasture, I would carefully construct a mansion. First, I pressed the tall grass down with my small feet outside of a carefully chosen rectangular perimeter. The bees and dragonflies often hovered curiously and moved on with their daily duties, but the music of their industriousness was the soundtrack of my imagination.

I worked diligently stomping the grass flat within the rectangle. First, the front door had to be placed to catch the morning sun as it rose from behind the Rocky Mountains to the east of our house. There would be large living rooms, bedrooms, a glorious kitchen and dining room, and always a nursery off the master bedroom.

Barry Manilow's *I Write the Songs*, Helen Reddy's *I Am Woman*, Linda Ronstadt, the BeeGees – these were songs I sang and hummed as I created my sacred space. I decorated my mansion with pheasant feathers, beautiful rocks, and other delights found within nature. I dreamed of being in love with my future husband. I pre-created the walls of love that would protect my future children. There was no limit to possibility.

In the fall of 2004, I was sweeping the floor of my five-thousand-square-foot dream home. ABBA's *The Winner Takes It All* was cranked as loud as I dared. Even though the neighbors were my best friends and would understand, I didn't want to attract attention. I was alone in that house that echoed with the words, "I don't want to talk about the things we've gone through. Though it's hurting me, now it's history."

The furniture was all loaded in the U-Haul parked in the driveway. My teenage son and preteen-aged son had walked to the new house. I had been able to find a rental within their school district that was not in a comfortable price range--but I felt the cost of too much change too fast could damage their already tender, aching psyches. My youngest son was eighteen months old. My neighbors had him next door, playing with their toddlers.

As I swept, each particle of dust, each scrunched and crackling piece of packing tape that ended up a frustrated ball of detritus, seemed spotlighted and larger than life. When I swept the last pile into the dustpan, the build-up of tension growing in my chest throughout the preceding months had nowhere else to expand. The excessive pressure caused a rupture that ripped through the walls I had built to contain my pain. A savage round of tears brought me down and I sat next to the dustpan and let the shards of my shattered life fall to the floor.

The years that followed were not always easy. I had tough choices to make, like all single mothers. I had to learn to balance my wants and desires as a woman with what was best for my children. Did I always make the right choice? No. But I always made the best decision at the time with the information I had. I learned to accept that and not beat myself up about mistakes.

Along that road of growth and recovery, I signed up for belly dancing classes. This investment in myself and the joy of movement sparked life into my dormant, creative self. Soon, I began dedicating time to small craft projects with the children and my creativity blossomed.

I cannot remember the exact date I found my inner child, but I do remember the glorious feeling of being transported back to the magical place where a small child made a mansion in the pasture and decorated it with pheasant feathers.

The decision to turn my life over to that state of being--one of full creativity with every faith in myself--was the best choice, bar none, post-divorce. I began to manifest the positive abundance I desired in my life through visualization, meditation, and detailed daydreams. I quit my twenty-five-year career in advertising and went back to university and enrolled in a creative writing program.

For the past six years, I have dedicated most of each day to learning how to capture and bask in the beautiful creativity that comes naturally to us as children. The innocent trust in my inner self, my soul's energy in expression, has transformed my world and brought me to a place of love and joy I never would have dreamed possible the day I thought I was broken beyond repair.

Today, spend half of each year in that dream house I mapped out in my child's mind. A beautiful Queen Anne built-in 1905 in the quaint seaside community of Gulfport, Florida. The other half of the year I live in a small village in Tuscany – the same village my paternal grandmother was born and raised in. I have created writing retreats for others looking to spark their creative magic and have been privileged to coach many of these beautiful souls in their path of creativity. I have had my poems published in renowned literary reviews and have completed my first novel. Along the way, I found a loving and supportive partner who encourages my creativity, as I support and encourage his creativity in the world of archeology.

I still search for feathers and beautiful stones. I place these throughout my house as a reminder of everything nature provides to us in limitless bounty. One floral arrangement, placed in front of my favorite window in my favorite room, sports three incandescent and elegant pheasant feathers.

Michele True,
Author, Poet, Writing Coach, and Pop-tart Addict.
michele@micheletrue.com

FOCUS 4

Relationships

"Many receive advice,
only the wise profit from it."

Harper Lee

Many major life transitions leave you lonely and isolated. For instance, changing jobs, losing someone, getting divorced, being an empty-nester, having a debilitating illness, and retiring from a job you love. Your loneliness and isolation can stem from literally being alone or feeling as though the people around you cannot relate to the changes you are going through. When I was thirty years old my father died. I felt disconnected from him my entire life, partly because he traveled all the time, but more so because he was a distant and abusive man. Although I had little contact with him, I was taken aback by how devastated I was by his death and what it took to move through it.

I needed support and connection with others. Many life transitions will leave you with the experience of FEELING LONELY & ISOLATED. Supportive, nurturing RELATIONSHIPS are key to getting through life transitions powerfully. Sometimes your current friends and family cannot or will not understand what you are experiencing, and you may be unclear on where to turn for the SUPPORT you need. However, you do it, you must find the right people to support your needs at this time in your life.

RELATIONSHIP is defined as the fact or state of having something in common, the state of having shared interests or efforts. The opposite of a relationship is disassociation.

It is critical that you have people in your life who share your interests and efforts and it is essential to guard against the tendency to hide out and lick your wounds. There are a number of ways to feel supported. Seek out communities, groups, and resources for connecting to new, supportive people in your life.

Some methods you can use to connect with others and relieve your feeling of loneliness and isolation are: hiring a therapist or coach, reading books on what you are dealing with, and searching the internet for online support and live support groups on the subject. Use the exercise below to support yourself in this endeavor and refer to Appendix A for some specific resources.

Getting Free Exercise

Step 1:

Search the internet for support communities related to the transition you are experiencing. (Entering adulthood, job loss, death or other loss, marriage, parenting, divorce, menopause, empty nest, health crisis, retirement, etc.)

Step 2:

Search Amazon for books related to the transition you are experiencing.

Step 3:

Consider hiring a therapist or coach to support you through the transition.

Step 4:

Search and join Meetup or Facebook communities that engage in activities and interests that match your vision.

How Brigette Reclaimed Her Life After Her Husband Cheated, Her Job Folded, and She Almost Ran Out of Money.

It was one of those years (or five) that read like a bad country song. My man cheated, the job folded, and the money damn near ran out. That was after my husband and I undertook a 2000-mile move to start over. It was spectacularly painful when I realized that we hadn't outrun our problems.

I'd wanted to believe that a change of scenery was the answer, but this implosion was the proverbial 2-4 between the eyes. It wasn't the first wake-up call, but it was the one that triggered me to clear away my make-it-work narrative. There was nothing else to do but walk away with my daughter, my dignity, and my yoga mat. I needed to get very, very clear on what I wanted...instead of settling for more of the same.

This was a pretty tall order in a new town, with a remote job...where I knew no one but my ex-husband, my daughter, and my sweet aunt. I realized quickly that I couldn't white-knuckle my way through and pretend that everything was on cruise control. I had a fierce band of girlfriends gathered from childhood, my pharmacy career, and yoga -teacher training community. These communities had been there for all the ups and downs, so I reached out. I didn't tell a tale of woe but requested their support to help me create something different this time. These women were successful, smart, willing to ask hard questions, and more than willing to visit my new desert, condo-home.

So, I let them. They came to hike, to create new pre-holiday rituals, to burn pieces of writing to release into the wind, but mostly just to be present. My aunt was generous in sharing the hard-won wisdom he'd gathered over her eighty years. We explored restaurants and hiking trails as we laughed and cried our way through the painful bits. I was finding my footing again. Shored up with my tribe of friends, I decided to create a new community for myself- determined to reinvent something good for my daughter and me. A yoga wall class called my name. For weeks, I braved learning to hang upside down and explored the edges of not knowing what to do. The teacher lovingly cooked for us and created a retreat space in her home. I joined meetup groups and braved online dating.

This feeling of being on firm ground continued to unfold as I entered coach training- where 1 learned how to deepen the relationship with myself... AND serve others. This knowledge cracked my worldwide open. I continued to create an intentional community and nurture that far-flung band of friends who always carried me through.

Years after that forced reset, life is richer than I could have envisioned. My circle has expanded again, to include a loving husband and larger family. I look back with gratitude for that time of learning how to ask for support, how to step out of my comfort zone, and how to learn to trust my footing--even when the path was unclear.

Brigette Serfaty, Integrative Health and Wellbeing Coach, Aligned Engagement Strategies,
https://aligned-engagement.com,
brigetteserfaty@gmail.com

FOCUS 5

Forgiveness and Healing

*"Step out of the history that is holding you back.
Step into the new story you are willing to
create."*

Oprah Winfrey

Difficult life transitions that we often think of as mistakes in judgment, poor choices or failures, often leave you feeling VERY EMBARRASSED.

You might think you are the only one who's been so _____! (Fill in the blank with the words or descriptions you say to yourself that are demeaning. Someone might say stupid, while others may say irresponsible.) Whatever your trigger word is, rest assured it is not who you truly are.

You tend to find a way to hide your pain, pretend everything is fine, and isolate yourself from friends and family. Human beings hate to admit when they are wrong and always want to appear as though they have it together.

The irony of this is, that when you allow yourself to be vulnerable and open, it permits others to do the same and allows true connections to blossom.

The antidote to embarrassment is usually FORGIVENESS which allows for deep HEALING.

FORGIVENESS is defined as a release from the guilt or penalty of an offense. The opposite of forgiveness is punishment and retribution.

It's close to impossible to move forward until you have forgiven yourself and/or another in situations where you want to punish or get retribution. Forgiving oneself and others is the most powerful tool we have for HEALING, moving on, and creating a new life.

The definition of HEALING is to make sound or whole, heal a wound, cause (an undesirable condition) to be overcome, or patch up or correct (a breach or division).

Getting Free Exercise

Begin by understanding that everyone makes mistakes in their lives. Agree to forgive yourself and others.

Engage in the following exercise of self-forgiveness.

Forgive Yourself

Step 1:

Identify the life choice or circumstance that you feel embarrassed about. (i.e. Marrying the wrong person).

Step 2:

Determine the reasons you made that choice at that time in your life.

Step 3:

If you were your best friend (someone who loved you unconditionally), what you would say to yourself to forgive yourself. Write this down, or better yet--write yourself a letter.

Step 4:

Reflect on and write down what you learned from your mistake. Plan to do something to celebrate what you learned from this life experience (take a candle-lit bubble bath, go to a spa and have a massage, go to dinner and a movie, etc.)

Step 5:

Create a statement of belief about yourself that empowers you. Say it to yourself in the mirror every day. (i.e. I am a beautiful, smart, vibrant woman who need not be embarrassed by my mistakes. I can be proud of my mistakes because they mean I have truly lived! My mistakes will bring me to the next place I need and want to be in my life, and I am proud of myself for recognizing my mistakes and learning from them.)

Forgive Others

Engage in the following exercise to forgive another. You can forgive someone without talking to them. This process is for you, not them. You can forgive someone who has passed away. It will make a difference for you if you can accept the situation and let it go.

Step 1:

Identify what the other did that hurt you or led to the life transition you find yourself in. (i.e. Spouse had an affair, etc.)

Step 2:

Imagine the reasons the person had for doing what they did.

Step 3:

If you were their best friend (someone who loves that person unconditionally), write down what you might say to him/her to forgive them. This does not have to make their behavior acceptable. It simply says, "I forgive you for doing what was unacceptable and still is."

Step 4:

Reflect on the value of holding on to the resentment toward that person. What is the secondary gain of it? By that, we mean, what is it that you gain from hanging on to the resentment? Can you use it to excuse yourself from powerfully moving on in your life?

Step 5:

Make a declaration of forgiveness. If it feels good, communicate your forgiveness. This could be in a letter, email, or in-person.

The Mother Paradox –
How Karen Overcame Difficulties with
Her Mother through Forgiveness

Ever watch a toddler at play? They explore the world for a bit and then run back to their mothers. Their mothers are their home base, their safe place. In her book Passages, Gail Sheehy, calls this behavior refueling. Little ones gain strength and reassurance from their mothers on their way to establishing physical and emotional independence. For parenting, independence is the goal, or at least it should be. The thing is it only starts in toddlerhood, when it is cute, seeking independence doesn't end there. As they get older it is no longer cute, it is deadly serious. Hence, the mother paradox, we yearn for our mother's support and reassurance at the same time we seek our independence.

Our relationships with our mothers are arguably our deepest, longest, and most formative. These relationships can also be the most confusing, frustrating, and challenging of our lives, especially when we are teenagers.

My parents were deeply religious and socially conservative. I was the 1950s, firstborn child and most significantly a girl. I was loved, even adored but that came with a price. They wanted to protect me from growing up too fast in the world where they had survived depression and a world war.

I was the Captain of the High School Speech Team, an officer in the Luther League; I taught Sunday school. babysat, did volunteer work, and was a church camp counselor. None of my "doing" was enough to prove myself worthy of a reasonable curfew or, and this was the kicker, learning how to drive a car. My parents had grown up in a major city that had a bus on the corner every thirty minutes. There were multiple trains downtown. You could go anywhere you wanted to go from parks and shopping to Wrigley Field or the Museum of Natural History. That was not true in newly constructed post-war suburbia, the only buses were school buses and the closest train was two towns over and an express train to Chicago's Loop. I was so screwed. All my peers drove. I had to beg rides that I could never reciprocate. I did not beg, I walked – long distances, on highways, at night, whatever it took to not draw attention to my inability to drive. If no one offered a ride I walked. I wasn't anything close to safe.

Injustice weighs heavy on a teenage heart.

Mom and I fought about driving, round after round. My dad was silent on the issue. I was merciless, I would press her when she was having her girlfriends over for lunch with one goal in mind, to embarrass her. The love was there but we didn't like each other much. I was eventually forbidden to use the word "car" in the house.

As I grew older, not knowing how to drive complicated my life immeasurably. When I finally convinced my husband to pay for driving lessons, I was seven months pregnant with my second child. My husband loved that I didn't drive, as with my parents, my lack of mobility was a tool of power and control. I did eventually divorce him but that took another decade.

Karen Koven is a poet and author. She received first place in the Romeo Lemay Poetry Competition. She has had several of her poems published in the Odet Journal as well as the Florida Bards Poetry Review.

Mastering Your Inner Critic

"Owning our story can be hard but not nearly as difficult as spending our lives running from it."

Brene Brown

You know you want to make a change; you have a vision for your future but that voice in your head that talks to you all day long keeps telling you, "You are crazy, that's too risky, it won't work out and you might look stupid, you are not smart enough, etc." This voice is your inner critic. Everyone has one and understanding, appreciating, and mastering your inner critic will serve you throughout your life.

The definition of a CRITIC is a person who judges, evaluates, or criticizes.

In this case, the critic is YOU. Often the original criticism came from an elder in our lives, yet the current criticism is you imposing this on yourself. Here's another point where the COURAGE we discussed earlier comes into play.

The opposite of a CRITIC is an ADVOCATE.

The definition of an ADVOCATE
supports or promotes the interests of another.
It's time to become your ADVOCATE.

Getting Free Exercise

Step 1:

Fill in the chart below. List the immediate thoughts you have from your inner critic and then choose the empowering thought you want as the foundation for your new life. For example, maybe your inner critic tells you something is too hard to accomplish. When this happens, choose to think of how life could be easy for you. After a while, you will notice that you pull this phrase into different situations whenever your inner critic tries to take over.

Topic	Inner Critic Thoughts	What I Choose to Think
Life		
Self		
Body		
Money		
Love/Rel.		
People		
Success		
God/Spirit		
Other		

Step 2:

Act "as if". Read the thoughts you have chosen to operate from and no matter how loud your inner critic gets, take actions and act "as if" the other were true. Dress like they are true, talk like they are true, and connect with people who will advocate for you when you can't advocate for yourself. If you act "as if" long enough, your negative inner critic will quiet down. This will take building muscle every day. They say it takes 10,000 hours of practice to master anything and I know you can do this because I have.

List ways you could act "as if".

(The exercises in this section are adapted from Mike Dooley's Infinite Possibilities Course (a course I am licensed to lead).

How Hilary Overcame Years of Depression by Mastering Her Inner Critic.

I was depressed for a long time when I was young. It began when I was thirteen, and we moved from a town near Toronto to a suburb of Montreal. I lost all my friends and I felt like I was in a different world--one I wasn't familiar with and that seemed fake. I felt alienated from my family. The suburban world we had landed in felt like a kind of desert. Life seemed meaningless. I started rebelling against my parents and they seemed to hate me, and I seemed to hate them. When I was sixteen, the doctor told me I was depressed.

There were a few glimmers of hope. When I was nineteen, I went to Vancouver with my boyfriend. For the first time, I encountered a different world and people with different perspectives. They seemed more authentic and had values I could connect with. My boyfriend and I were picking fruit for the summer in the Okanagan Valley and I spent that time debating whether I was going to stay in British Columbia or go back east. I struggled with that decision for the entire summer. In the end, I didn't have the self-confidence to listen to what my heart was telling me to do. I returned home and began my second year of university, studying biology. I immediately fell back into a depression and then decided, "okay, let's just get through this darn thing," and I finished university.

I chose to travel in my twenties because I kept asking, "Why am I here? What's my purpose? What is this world? Is this all there is?" My boyfriend and I bought one-way tickets to New Delhi, India, where we had a great adventure. When we ran out of money, we went to Japan and taught English. From there we ventured to

Australia, where my aunt and uncle lived. And then, we split up. Later I moved to England.

During this time of travel, my life was kind of up and down. When I was feeling excited about things, it was an adventure, so I was happy. But then as soon as I went to England, I felt depressed again. The grayness of the place got to me. I didn't know what I wanted to do with my life and I wondered "what am I doing here?" There was always a sense of meaningfulness ingrained within the depression. That's when I started to have wild moods, swinging from manic to depressive. It was a roller coaster. I used coffee to amp up and alcohol to bring me down again.

Then I encountered somebody who was my huge lifesaver. She was an acupuncturist, and her healing shifted my life. She practiced Traditional Chinese Medicine and said my fire energy was drowned out by my water energy. I saw her for two years and our work balanced my moods. I was no longer in the up and down, chaotic roller coaster where I couldn't get much done.

I encountered a situation, then, that triggered my insomnia. I had not learned the lesson of listening to my inner self. I kept searching for my path in life and what I wanted to do. During this early phase in London, I was exploring all of these possibilities. I spent a year studying fine art and also counseling, which I loved. And then I thought, "okay, now it's time to have a real-life profession."

I was very drawn to study counseling. It was clear this was my gift, using my empathy and natural ability to understand people. But I didn't go there. Instead, I decided to be a schoolteacher.

The night before my practicum, I couldn't sleep. That triggered a problem with sleeplessness that lasted for years. I had truly abandoned my soul path. I was twenty-seven, had experienced traveling the world, and had encountered something I loved. Yet, I didn't choose it. I chose something very conventional. This sent me into another deep depression.

I moved to Toronto and got a job as a high school science teacher where I taught for two years. However, this role did not suit me at all.

Luckily, I stumbled into organizational training as a profession, and I started to feel much more in my natural world. I was designing and delivering courses that helped people get insight into who they are. From there I became a facilitator and worked with groups on how to function well together. I was expressing my natural gifts in a different setting. I started to take psychology courses, again and applied what I was learning to my work. I had finally found my true calling and my true path.

I think the critical voice was very much present throughout my life, which is why I struggled to listen to my heart. It was also the source of my depression--along with straying from my soul path. I wasn't aware of this critical voice, I simply followed its orders.

At some point, I came across some tools that brought me out of depression. The first tool was Martin Seligman's theories on positive psychology which describes optimistic and pessimistic patterns. I started noticing those patterns in myself.

Another tool that helped me was Rick Carson's book, Taming Your Gremlin, which is a great metaphor for that inner critic. I became very adept overtime at cutting off that critical voice and not listening to it. I was excited about the whole notion of mental mastery and how you can have choices about your mental patterns, and train yourself to think differently.

I rarely get depressed anymore and I sleep easily. I am in touch with my purpose and doing work I love. I manage my inner critic with the many tools I have developed over the years. I trust my inner voice and listen to my heart.

Hillary Samuel is a health coach and sleep expert. She helps people get great sleep.

hilary@asleepatlast.com

www.AsleepAtLast.com

(613) 686-3113

FOCUS 7

Connecting with Source

"The cosmos is within us.
We are made of star-stuff.
We are a way for the universe to know itself."

Carl Sagan

What is the source in your life? I am referring to whatever spiritual connection you have to the universe. If you are a religious person, you may connect with God, Jesus, Buddha, or some other entity. If you are not religious, you may connect through nature, the universe, the eternal, philosophy, or academic study. Regardless of how you connect, it is important to have a place to go that makes you feel grounded in both the world and in yourself.

The definition of SOURCE is a generative force or cause, a point of origin or procurement/beginning.

The opposite of SOURCE is DEAD or CLOSING.

It is critical when experiencing a life transition that we find a place of SOURCE. A new beginning that generates a new life.

Getting Free Exercise

Step 1:

Find a practice that connects you to your source. If you are religious, attend services consistently. Make sure you are connecting with your spiritual source, not just going through the motions. Join study groups at your place of worship that stimulate your spiritual life and also act as a support community.

If you are not religious, find rituals that connect you with your source. This might include reading and studying spiritual books, joining study groups, or working with oracle cards, etc.

Step 2:

Learn to meditate at least ten minutes a day. Sitting in silence, breathing, and being focused on connecting with your inner self has been proven to assist in getting and staying grounded. A great resource is a book *The Miracle Morning* by Hal Elrod. See the appendix for more resources, both written, and audio/visual.

Step 3:

Keep a gratitude journal. It is too easy to focus on what you don't have than to focus on what you are grateful for. When you focus on what you are grateful for, you attract more of it. A fantastic book and program I recommend is *The Magic* by Rhonda Byrne.

How Fern Overcame a Series of Devastating Changes by Connecting with Her Source.

A series of significant, life-changing events happened to me over a few years. These led me to a lot of existential questions, and on a spiritual path.

Here's what happened. I initiated a divorce and just as I was beginning to feel comfortable with my singleness and independence, my daughter went off to college on the other side of the country.

After she left, the structure of my life collapsed. For the past eighteen years, I had someone to take care of. I scheduled my life around her needs, activities, school, then suddenly all of that was gone. The first year, I worried obsessively about her safety--was she eating enough? Were people taking advantage of her generous spirit?

Anything and everything was up for worry. I suffered from insomnia, and I was hanging out with people who partied and drank too much.

My daughter and I talked almost daily and those times were precious. Oftentimes she would call me before she set off to class.

One day, I was feeling my misery and realizing that my lifestyle did not support happiness. I had to figure out how to fill the hole in my heart and life, the one left gaping open after my daughter, who previously filled everything in me to overflowing, moved out.

When I was married, I remember reading a book by the Dali Lama and that led me to learn more about Buddhism and I started reading books, meditating, and practicing mindfulness. I went to talks and group meditations at the local Buddhist temple.

I learned that happiness is within and starts with self-love. When you don't have that strong foundational strength within yourself, it's easy to be swayed to follow anything that might make you temporarily happy. I spent a couple of years doing internal work. It wasn't easy and it brought up a lot of unpleasant emotions and memories that I had to process to arrive at a stable, foundational core of being.

Then I met someone. It was a really happy time, but after a couple of years, he died unexpectedly in his sleep. When I received the call, I was devastated, and that day still lives in my memory.

Even as I write this, tears fill my eyes. That grief stayed with me for a couple of years and having my spiritual practice turn to help with the process a lot. His mother gave me one of the Persian rugs she owned. I used to meditate on it to connect with him. I cherish it as much as the memories we had together.

Without my spiritual practices, this second and enormous loss could have destroyed me. However, I was able to find peace in my life by turning toward spirituality.

Fern Carbonell, INHC, Midlife Wellness Coach and Mediation Guide

FOCUS 8

Taking Action
in the Real World

*"The most difficult thing is the decision to act,
the rest is merely tenacity."*

Amelia Earhart

You have gotten clarity on your values and vision for the future. You've found the courage, trust, belief, and bravery to move forward. You feel creative and have the relationships you need around you. You have forgiven yourself and others, have begun to master your inner critic and feel connected with your source. Now what?

Now it's time to make your MASTER PLAN. You can think and dream and meditate and visualize – all of which is valuable – for days, weeks, months, or years without ever getting to where you want to be. In the real world, you must always take action – the right actions – to make something happen. I have taken all the elements discussed in the past nine sections and developed a master plan for you to work from.

Getting Free Exercise

Now, can you fill out this MASTER PLAN using the work you have completed in the previous sections with the addition of your action plan in time.

Master Plan Date: _____

My Vision is:

My Key Values are:

What I want to accomplish is:

The empowering belief I have is:

My support communities are:

The inner critic messages I will reject are:

I will stay connected with my inner source by practicing the following:

The actions I will take to achieve my goal(s) are:

Action   **by When (Date)**

1.

2.

3.

4.

5.

6.

7.

8.

9.

10.

There is an art and science to effective planning time management. If you would like to become more proficient, consider joining one of my weekly Sage Support Groups and ordering my planning system. Mastering your time is a powerful aspect of mastering your life.

How Jenn Pulled Off a Miracle: to Have Her Home Birth in Her New Home (Which Wasn't Possible Because She Was Homeless.)

When I was about thirty-four, I found myself in a position I didn't think I'd be in....pregnant with my third kid, unemployed, and homeless.

Now, I know that paints a pretty dark picture. It was a challenging situation, but it was lined with hope. You see, at the time my small family, which included my husband Kevin and our two children, had been traveling the US while living full time in our RV. My father suddenly passed away, which compelled us to settle down and get grounded.

We moved in with my in-laws and the day after we sold our RV, we learned that we were pregnant with our third child. In the wake of my dad's passing, this was a true blessing.

But then shit got real! My only income came from traveling to California for work, and soon the pregnancy would keep me from flying.

What complicated matters is that I was determined to have a home birth – even if I didn't have a home of my own. In the middle of the second trimester, our midwives asked where we planned to give birth. YIKES!

I stood up in their office, stomped my foot on the ground, and said, "Mark my words, we will be in our own house before this baby is born!"

Woah, how were we going to do this? My husband had just started a new business, and I had one more gig in California. Our credit card debt was growing, and we didn't have a conventional background, so that eliminated most rental and mortgage options.

I did the one thing I'd done in the past that made a difference: visualization. I know it sounds cheesy and believe me there was more to it than picturing rainbows and butterflies. But seriously, every day I would go for a walk and repeat to myself: "I will have a healthy and peaceful birth in our own beautiful and spacious home."

Then we began living "as if". As if we could buy a house, as if we had a stable business, as if we were preparing for a home birth, and as if I was a profitable coach. We began touring houses for sale in a thirty-mile radius, I began coaching, and my husband dedicated himself to learning the ropes of his business.

We were down to the wire with about six weeks left. One of my in-law's neighbors had become a friend and was willing to take her house off the market and rent to us with the agreement we would eventually take ownership. But we still didn't have the money for rent and deposit, let alone living expenses.

That month, I sold more coaching packages than ever before, Kevin's business was becoming profitable, and we were making bold moves. I reached out to friends and family offering donation-based coaching sessions. A dear friend reminded me that I didn't have to know HOW the money could come for our home, just that we do everything in our power (legally of course) to manifest the money, and then ACCEPT the abundance.

That donation-based offer, which was SO FAR OUT of my comfort zone, brought in enough money to cover our deposit and first month's rent. On May 5, 2018, we signed a lease agreement and were handed the keys to our house. Our daughter was born in our beautiful and spacious home on May 26th.

After another series of bold moves and hard work, we signed a contract taking ownership of our home on Feb 5, 2021. By taking action, visualizing our desired outcome, and believing that we would be provided for, we are happily on the road to fulfilling our big, life vision.

Jenn Schmidt
Hiring Manager & Mortgage Protection Specialist
jennsfglife@gmail.com
563.542.8325
https://schmidtgroupsfg.com/

CONCLUSION

You are a magnificent human being, living a life filled with challenges and triumphs. You deserve everything that love and life have to offer, and it is my mission to help anyone I cross paths with to live a life full of joy, freedom, and satisfaction. Whatever hardships you have or are suffering exist to lead you to a new level of happiness and satisfaction.

All you need to do is put in the work of getting clear and generating the courage to take the next steps. You may be unsure of where those next steps may lead you but believe that they will lead you in the right direction.

I am available now or in the future to assist you in resolving limiting beliefs, healing past trauma, engaging in forgiveness, and designing and implementing your next chapter. Know that you are loved and supported. You only need to ask and accept. I know that you have what it takes and can overcome any fears that try to stop you. When you are ready to blast off, give me a call.

With deep love and respect,

Patti

Appendix

The following examples and information are meant to clarify and inspire you to complete the moving forward exercises in this book. Please feel free to drop me a line at patti@sagethink.com and let me know how you are progressing or to ask me any questions you might have.

Write a "10 Years from Now" Letter

You can write this letter or description from any perspective. Just play with it and make sure it excites you. You may not achieve everything you write about, but you will move toward it and achieve much of it. Here is a sample:

I am now making $500,000 or more reliably and easily each year. My best-selling books have made me known the world over and I work with ten VIP clients per year. My quarterly programs and ongoing packages are now delivered by my brilliant staff and are known for making absurdly positive impacts on other's lives. My foundation keeps growing and saving other's lives. I have two incredible grandchildren that I care for two days a week and my daughter's business keeps expanding in sync with mine. I am healthy and fit and can see my way to living to one-hundred years of age. I love art and have discovered ways to express my creative talents. My husband and I travel to Europe several times a year for his photography, and I am ready to publish my third novel.

I awake each morning to the sound of the birds chirping outside my window. I gaze out upon the pool and can see the sun rising over the Gulf of Mexico. I hop out of bed with the energy of a twenty-year-old and engage in my morning routine of meditation, journaling, reading, and stretching, followed by a brisk walk on the beach. When I return, my assistant has prepared my breakfast and as I read my email, I see that my bank account has grown overnight. I do love my passive income. My husband greets me with a kiss and I have a sweet good morning text from my daughter asking when we can meet. After getting the week planned with my daughter, I settle into working on my 4th novel. I am excited to see what my character, Julianna, is up to next. Around 5 pm, our grandchildren descend upon us and we begin to play as though we were children again. They are the sunshine of my existence, and I am so happy we have the means to care for them. As the day draws to a close, I feel a sense of deep happiness and satisfaction.

Resources

Please note: I have used some of the resources listed here and not others. I have researched the resources and determined I would probably use that resource if and when I needed them. You may find many other resources by searching for books and communities specific to your values.

ABANDONMENT & LOSS

The Journey from Abandonment to Healing: Revised and Updated: Surviving Through and Recovering from the Five Stages That Accompany the Loss of Love by Susan Anderson.

The Abandonment Recovery Workbook: Guidance through the Five Stages of Healing from Abandonment, Heartbreak, and Loss by Susan Anderson

The Grief Recovery Handbook, 20th Anniversary Expanded Edition: The Action Program for Moving Beyond Death, Divorce, and Other Losses including Health, Career, and Faith by John W. James and Russell Friedman

Support Communities:

https://www.griefrecoverymethod.com/our-programs/1-on-1-online-support

CAREER & JOB SEARCH

What Color Is Your Parachute? 2021: Your Guide to a Lifetime of Meaningful Work and Career Success Paperback – December 22, 2020 by Richard N. Bolles (Author), Katharine Brooks EdD (Author)

The Two Hour Job Search by Steve Dalton

MARRIAGE

The Couple's Activity Book: 70 Interactive Games to Strengthen Your Relationship Paperback - September 22, 2020 by Crystal Schwanke (Author)

A Year of Us: A Couples Journal: One Question a Day to Spark Fun and Meaningful Conversations Paperback - June 18, 2019 by Alicia Muñoz LPC (Author)

Our Bucket List: A Creative and Inspirational Journal for Ideas and Adventures for Couples Paperback - February 16, 2018 by Lux Reads (Author)

CHILDBIRTH

The First-Time Mom's Pregnancy Handbook: A Week-by-Week Guide from Conception through Baby's First 3 Months by Bryn Huntpalmer and Stuart J. Fischbein MD FACOG | Dec 3, 2019

The Baby Owner's Manual: Operating Instructions, Trouble-Shooting Tips, and Advice on First-Year Maintenance (Owner's and Instruction Manual) Book 1 of 11: Owner's and Instruction Manual | by Louis Borgenicht M.D. and Joe Borgenicht | Sep 10, 2012

Becoming the Parent You Want to Be: A Sourcebook of Strategies for the First Five Years by Laura Davis and Janis Keyser | Feb 3, 1997

RAISING TEENAGERS

Get Out of My Life, but First Could You Drive Me & Cheryl to the Mall: A Parent's Guide to the New Teenager, Revised and Updated by Anthony E. Wolf | Aug 21, 2002

*This was my bible during my daughter's teen years.

DIVORCE

Your Healthy Divorce Journey: A Step-by-Step Guide Through the Process of Divorce by Erica R. Ellis

The Divorce Planner Checklist: Navigate and Negotiate Your Way to an Optimum Outcome by Laura Campbell and with Lili Vasileff

The Empowered Woman's Guide to Divorce: A Therapist and a Lawyer Guide You Through Your Divorce Journey by Jill Murray PsyD and Adam Dodge JD

NEGOTIATING ILLNESS

Dropping Wood, Spilling Water: Illness, Disability, and Aging as Paths for Consciousness and Being Paperback by Robert Shuman

Lucky Man: A Memoir by Michael J Fox

Surviving and Thriving with an Invisible Chronic Illness (How to Stay Sane and Live One Step Ahead of Your Symptoms) Paperback - by Ilana Jacqueline

The Things We Don't Say: An Anthology of Chronic Illness Truths Paperback - by Julie Morgenlender

Dancing with Elephants: Mindfulness Training for Those Living With Dementia, Chronic Illness or an Aging Brain (How to Die Smiling Series) (Volume 1) by Jarem Sawatsky

SPIRITUAL RENEWAL

Dynamics of Spiritual Life: An Evangelical Theology of Renewal by Richard F. Lovelace

The Rituals & Practices of a Jewish Life: A Handbook for Personal Spiritual Renewal by Rabbi Kerry M. Olitzky

Spiritual Gems of Islam: Insights &Practices from the Qur'an, Hadith, Rumi & Muslim Teaching Stories to Enlighten the Heart & Mind by Imam Jamal Rahman

The Heart of the Buddha's Teaching: Transforming Suffering into Peace, Joy, and Liberation Thich Nhat Hanh

Elegant Prayer Journal: Nondenominational Prayer Journal Diary Notebook by Niall Graham

Spirituality Before Religions: Spirituality is Unseen Science... Science is Seen Spirituality by Kaba Hiawatha Kamene

PSYCH-K®...The Missing Peace In Your Life! by Robert K. Williams

The Biology of Belief 10th Anniversary Edition: Unleashing the Power of Consciousness, Matter & Miracles by Bruce H. Lipton

FORGIVENESS

Radical Self-Forgiveness: The Direct Path to True Self-Acceptance by Colin Tipping

Dead Set on Living: Making the Difficult but Beautiful Journey from F#*king Up to Waking Up by Chris Grosso
The Self Forgiveness Handbook by Thom Rutledge

Forgiving What You Can't Forget: Discover How to Move On, Make Peace with Painful Memories, and Create a Life That's Beautiful Again by Lysa TerKeurst

Forgiving Others, Forgiving Ourselves: Understanding and Healing Our Emotional Wounds by Myra Warren Isenhart Ph.D. and Michael Spangle Ph.D.

The Secret of Lasting Forgiveness: How To Find Peace By Forgiving Others and Yourself by Bruce Wilkinson and Mark E. Strong

SELF-ESTEEM

The Gifts of Imperfection: Let Go of Who You Think You're Supposed to Be and Embrace Who You Are by Brene' Brown

Self-Love Workbook for Women: Release Self-Doubt, Build Self-Compassion, and Embrace Who You Are by Megan Logan MSW LCSW

You Are a Badass: How to Stop Doubting Your Greatness and Start Living an Awesome Life by Jen Sincero

I found that researching books and online resources for this book to be exciting. I wanted to devour the information. I recommend you search until you find the resources that spark you to move forward in your life. Don't ever give up on yourself.

I have found being in my sixties to be the most exhilarating and satisfying time of my life. I am learning and discovering new things every day and I appreciate all that my life has given me and taught me.

I plan to live into my nineties, and I am ready to transform anything life throws at me.

If you know you need support or just want to discover the next right thing in your life, go to www.sagethink.com and schedule a FREE discovery session.

With love,
Patti

Epilogue

You were born.

You deserve to succeed because you were born.

You belong because you were born.

You are loved and lovable because you were born.

Life is your game to play.

Challenges allow you to grow and learn.

Mistakes are inevitable.

Pain and heartbreak are inevitable.

Joy and satisfaction come when you stop resisting.

The universe is longing to give you what you desire.

You have what you need at your fingertips.

Let it in.

At any moment, in any situation, at any age, your life can transform.

Support exists.

Go find it.

Love yourself above all else.

And make space for others to love themselves.

You are one with all things and you alone can make the difference.

Own yourself and go impact your life and the universe.

Acknowledgments

The journey to write this book has taken over four years. The first person I would like to thank is Nancy Erickson, The Book Professor. She was my first writing coach and taught me how to plan, write and polish my first draft. I spent two years in writing groups with her and she supported me to keep going despite my cancer diagnosis. Our work together was invaluable.

Next, I want to acknowledge my dear friend, Karen Koven, for introducing me to my next writing coach and editor, Michele True. Michele helped me see what was strong about my writing and where I needed to tweak or add content. Working with her has been amazing.

In addition, I want to thank my best friends, Deb, Kelley, Karen, and Sara, for encouraging me, reading the book before publication, and giving me valuable feedback.

I also want to thank my writing group, Barbara, Allie, and Janet as well as Michele's open mic for allowing me to read sections to them and critiquing my work.

In addition, I want to thank my dear friends Nancy, Karen, Michele, Hilary, Brigette, Christina, Fern, and Jenn for writing their stories of triumph. Each of them inspires me daily.

Another incredible support was my formatter and friend, Tonja Waring for putting the final touches on the book and helped me actually publish it.

Finally, I want to thank my brother and sisters for supporting me throughout my life as I moved through many difficult transitions and last but most importantly, my amazing husband, Andrew, and daughter, Matilda for loving me always and being proud of who I am and what I produce in the world.

Made in the USA
Columbia, SC
14 July 2021